*The Authentic Bars, Cafés
and Restaurants of Buenos Aires*

The Authentic Bars,
Cafés and Restaurants of

BUENOS AIRES

....

Gabriela Kogan

THE LITTLE BOOKROOM
NEW YORK

© 2007 Gabriela Kogan
Assistant: Marina Kogan
Photographs © 2007 Gabriela Kogan
Map © 2007 Gabriela Kogan
(Vicente Restaurante: Camila Miyazono Lopez)
Translation © Mariana Mamelink

Book design: Louise Fili Ltd.

Manufactured in Mexico.

Library of Congress Cataloging-in-Publication Data

Kogan, Gabriela, 1967-
The authentic bars, cafés and restaurants of Buenos Aires / by Gabriela Kogan.
p. cm.
Includes index.
ISBN 1-892145-55-3 (alk. paper)
1. Restaurants—Argentina—Buenos Aires—Guidebooks.
2. Bars (Drinking establishments)—Argentina—Buenos Aires—Guidebooks.
3. Buenos Aires (Argentina)—Guidebooks. I. Title.
TX907.5.A72K64 2008
647.9582'11—dc22
2007040131

Published by The Little Bookroom
435 Hudson Street, 3rd floor
New York NY 10014
editorial@littlebookroom.com
www.littlebookroom.com
Distributed by Random House, in the UK
and Ireland by Signature Book Services, and throughout
the world (except for Central and South America)
by Random House International.

CONTENTS

INTRODUCTION

THERE ARE MANY WAYS TO GET TO KNOW BUENOS AIRES, BUT THERE ARE ONLY A FEW DOORS INTO ITS HEART. THE cafés, bars, and restaurants of the city grant easy entrée to the city's true spirit. They are where the customs and traditions of those who live their everyday lives to the fullest in Buenos Aires and who build their identities as *porteños* (residents of Buenos Aires) can still be found.

Buenos Aires has a long history of visitors—those who established the city (not once, but twice), those who came in the waves of immigration, those who left, those who were made to leave, and those who have tried to leave but have been lured back. Many people came to Buenos Aires on their own, with a suitcase full of traditions and dreams, with culinary secrets and a hunger for the future. Perhaps that's why so many of the establishments profiled here became vital places for meetings between expats, and part of the myth of the city. A large part of the life of this city takes place in its cafés and bars. They are the ideal settings for chats, confessions, and informal meetings, and they grant permission to unpack dreams from that suitcase.

In Buenos Aires, you will find cafés, bars, and café-bars. In all of them, you can get very good espresso (or something stronger). If bars and cafés were meant to provide distinct social environments, their subsequent combination has created yet another singular experience with its own atmosphere.

Bars and cafés had different moments of glory in the history of the city. Up until the nineteen seventies, every block in Buenos Aires had its own café and its own neighborhood corner bar—this has unfortunately been changing due to gentrification, economic crises, and the closing of long-standing family businesses that are no longer viable. Bars became default meeting places, mainly for men, who passed the time in literary and political debate—a key element of Argentine "café culture." Women were typically forbidden from bars unless accompanied by their husbands in a dining area set apart from the saloon. In the sixties and seventies, during Argentina's period of women's liberation, women began enrolling, en masse, in universities and began to participate in politics, making the bar a more equal-opportunity hangout. In the seventies, military rule forbade public meetings of more than two people for fear of political conspiracy, and raids on bars and cafés sapped the life out of many favorite institutions. More recently, many neighborhoods are losing those characteristics that make them unique, details that fuel the character and spirit of so many cafés and bars.

Nearly all cafés and bars were founded by Spanish immigrants, the largest immigrant community to arrive during the twentieth century, and they instilled their establishments with a unique style and rhythm. Like almost everything else in this city, restaurants were established by immigrants, too, but in the case of eateries, the founders were mainly from Italy. It didn't take long for them to make Argentina home, and today it's impossible to separate Italian from Argentine traditions. So, Sunday means pasta and family meals. Restaurants open themselves up like private homes. Perhaps because immigrants fled from a time of strife and hunger in Europe, restaurant meals in Buenos Aires are characterized by abundance, high-quality food, and, for those who immi-

grated here for serenity and a future, merriment.

Visiting these places and writing these brief descriptions, I realized that I began to retell and relive what Buenos Aires is really like, its history in all of its idiosyncrasy. The establishments included in this book have weathered some of the worst political and economic crises South America has ever seen, and perhaps that is why they represent the Argentine soul so well. They are timeless places, having found the mysterious formula to remain untouched by time. All these places are so important in the lives of the city's residents that it is impossible to imagine Buenos Aires without them. They are the meeting places, hangouts, and storied restaurants for *porteños* and visitors alike. But, above all, writing this guide has connected me to the joy of what is genuine, of what doesn't need language to translate. It has connected me to the essence of Buenos Aires.

Buenos Aires is a welcoming city. It has always held its arms wide open, and these establishments are its ambassadors. For those who haven't visited Buenos Aires, this book is an open invitation! Come savor its places, its food; meet its people at these cafés and experience what is at once sublime and routine. To those who live in this city that we love, let's celebrate it! Let's overcrowd its bars, its cafés, its restaurants and let's propose a toast to what makes us unique, to what defines us, and to what constitutes the purest part of our identity. And, as Italo Calvino says in *Invisible Cities*, "Let's learn how to make it last and leave it space."

—Gabriela Kogan

NOTE: Listings are organized by neighborhood. Hours are listed as they are traditionally in Buenos Aires. For some guidance, lunch is usually served between noon and 4pm and dinner between 8pm and 1am. You may want to call in advance to confirm opening hours to avoid any disappointment. Tips of around 10 percent are customary, and in these establishments, typically given in cash. If you would like a taxi on leaving, simply ask the cashier to call for you, as is customary. Dishes that appear in italics can be found in the glossary on page 152.

CONFECTIONER LAS VIOLETAS

Confectioner – Restaurant

....

AV. RIVADAVIA *3899* ~ ALMAGRO

☎ *4958.7387*

MONDAY *to* THURSDAY: 6AM *to* 2AM

FRIDAY *to* SUNDAY: 24 HOURS

MORE THAN 120 YEARS AGO, CONFECTIONER LAS VIO-
LETAS OPENED RIGHT IN THE HEART OF THE ALMAGRO.
Since then, it has been famous for its cakes and for its art
nouveau stained glass imported from France in 1884. Las Violetas
attracted not just locals, but the most famous celebrities from the world
of culture: poet Alfonsina Storni, writer Roberto Arlt, former president
Arturo Frondizi, socialist leader Nicolás Repetto, and the country's most
famous tango singer, Carlos Gardel.

When it closed its doors in 1998 for remodeling, a group of locals
managed to collect more than 10,000 signatures so that it might
be declared a "place of national interest"; thanks to this designation,
the original architecture and Las Violetas' unique style have been
preserved.

During the day, you can sample coffee and croissants or toasted sandwiches, and at lunch the food typical of a stylish restaurant. Drinks and
cocktails served with *ingredientes* (bar snacks) are a must for those at the

end of their workday or those just starting their evenings out. At night, the à la carte menu allows you to choose among a variety of Argentine dishes with international touches, like *mollejas de corazón al verdeo*, *bondiola a la riojana*, *lomo de bife Las Violetas*, or interesting options of pasta and fish. For dessert, one must order *copas heladas*, a typical Buenos Airean dessert.

On weekends, tea time is celebrated in the old way, featuring the well-known house patisserie. It's best is to order the *té La Violetera*, a tray to share of *masas finas* (fancy cookies), sandwiches, puddings, *pan dulce* (panettone), toast, and cake, with a pot of tea of your choosing.

Against the large windows overlooking Avenida Rivadavia is a patisserie selection in the best French style where pastry lovers can buy *masas finas*, chocolates, and cakes elegantly exhibited in the shop's original showcases.

The backdrop of many films, Las Violetas, with its great tearoom and famous windows, preserves memorable tales from the times when there was still a room reserved for families and a balcony for the belle époque-style ladies orchestra at tea time.

EL BANDERÍN

Café

. . . .

GUARDIA VIEJA *3601* ~ ALMAGRO

☏ *4862.7757*

MONDAY *to* FRIDAY: 8AM *to* 8PM

EL BANDERÍN IS LOCATED WHERE THE BOUNDARY BETWEEN ALMAGRO AND ABASTO BLURS. JUST AS ITS NAME IMPLIES, the flags, or pennants—over 400 of them—of football teams from all over the world and from all eras hang on the walls of the bar, along with photographs of the famous characters who have honored the bar with their presence.

Nowadays, El Banderín is frequented by writers and philosophy students from the Universidad de Buenos Aires, in addition to the locals who enjoy the familiarity of the neighborhood. When you order a sandwich, the meats are cut on an old-fashioned slicer on the bar, in front of everyone.

Its big glass windows brighten the room during the day, making it ideal for reading the newspaper over a coffee. In summer, there

are also tables on the sidewalk. El Banderín, in the heart of Buenos Aires, is equidistant between Avenida Córdoba and Avenida Corrientes, and is the perfect place for a coffee with friends, a chat about football, or to read for a while in a quiet, yet lively, atmosphere.

LA ORQUÍDEA

Café

. . . .

AV. CORRIENTES *4101* ~ ALMAGRO

☎ *4864.0957*

24 HOURS

LOCATED ON THE CORNER OF CORRIENTES AND ACUÑA DE FIGUEROA, LA ORQUÍDEA OWES ITS NAME TO THE flower market that stood opposite this traditional café until 2002. Since the market opened very early in the morning, La Orquídea was, and is, open twenty-four hours a day, which makes it the only bar in the neighborhood available for sleepless customers and night birds. So it is the perfect choice for university students, writers, and taxi drivers.

During the day, it is common to find visitors reading the paper, teachers and students from the Universidad de Buenos Aires using it as a hangout and, to give it a different touch entirely, couples anxiously awaiting pregnancy test results from the institute at the other end of the street.

La Orquídea is timeless, eternal; it belongs to the neighborhood. That's the feeling of regular customers, who—according to the owner—"have been the same for fifty years."

Famous for its *milanesas* with salad, mashed potatoes, or french fries, the menu is admittedly a tad limited. The most popular items are coffee, croissants, toasted sandwiches, and *picadas*.

The tables next to the windows are always the first to be taken by those losing themselves in thought; watching, as Jorge Schucheim's song goes, "Buenos Aires go past and past."

MIRAMAR

Restaurant / Rotisería

. . . .

AV. SAN JUAN *1999* ~ BALVANERA

☎ *4304.4261*

WEDNESDAY *to* MONDAY: 11AM *to* 11:30PM

CLOSED TUESDAYS

AT FIRST SIGHT, MIRAMAR LOOKS LIKE A TYPICAL LOCAL BODEGÓN, ONE OF THE LAST FEW LEFT, WITH A *ROTISERÍA* (deli), accessed through another door in the corner. But once you are inside, the options on the menu and what you see on the impeccable white-tableclothed tables will still surprise you. Apart from the famous cold cuts and prepared nibbles, the special character of the place lies in the choice of snails, frogs, partridges, oysters, rabbit, and anchovies, among other exquisite local delicacies.

Unless you are dining alone, I recommend that you order many different dishes to sample the varied menu offerings, though it is common to see solo customers eating a traditional dish. The wine list is one of the most varied in the city.

Many years ago there was a hat factory here and tango legend Carlos Gardel, who always had his hat on, of course, used to be a customer. Nowadays, as fate would have it, tango singers fill the place with their music every Sunday night, imbuing the restaurant and the food with the spirit of Buenos Aires.

ROMA

Café

....

SAN LUIS *3101* ~ BALVANERA

☎ *4961.8863*

DAILY IN WINTER: 6:30AM *to* 8:30PM

SUMMER HOURS VARY

"**T**HE CAFÉ ON THE CORNER" IS A DEEPLY ROOTED TRADITION IN BUENOS AIRES, LIKE TANGO OR AVENIDA CORRIENTES. IF somebody wants to know what a typical neighborhood café is like, they have to look no further than Roma. It has remained unchanged for more than fifty years; its owner, who on arriving from Spain, decided to keep the name of the café that formerly occupied the site. He liked it so much the way it was he kept the large painting of General San Martín as the room's focal point, along with the bottles of wine from all eras of the café's history that cover the walls. They simply remained there waiting to be opened, and time has made them the distinctive mark of the café.

The menu consists of only sandwiches and, of course, white coffee, and croissants or a *cortado* served in a small glass during the day, and *picadas* with beer or gin at

sunset. The most important aspect of places like this is the atmosphere. The same tables are always taken by the same customers, or at least it seems that way. The moment you walk into Roma, you are immediately part of it: its windows, its aroma, the community of regulars and friends. How many places like this are there in Buenos Aires? Countless. They were born with Spanish immigrants, grew with the customary chats between neighbors, and lived on to become the unmistakable mark of a city that celebrates meetings between friends, even if they have moved from the neighborhood.

EL SANJUANINO

Home Cooking

....

S. DE BUSTAMANTE *1788* ~ BARRIO NORTE

☎ *4822.8080*

POSADAS *1515* ~ RECOLETA

☎ *4804.2909*

TUESDAY *to* SUNDAY: 11:30AM *to* 3PM *and* 7PM *to* MIDNIGHT

EMPANADAS AND ASADO ARE THE MOST POPULAR TRADITIONAL DISHES IN ARGENTINA. EACH PART OF THE COUNTRY has its own distinct version which fills those who make them with national and regional pride. The pre-Andean region of Cuyo, lodged

between the desert and the vineyards, has its best proponent in El Sanjuanino. This little restaurant preserves the region's culinary traditions and combines a warm country atmosphere with a high level of cooking. The highlights are empanadas *criollas, tamales, humitas,* and *locro*—perhaps the most emblematic dish of the countryside. All these typical inland dishes find their urban interpretation here, with the exact spices and special touches that make this restaurant unique. Tra-

ditional desserts do not disappoint either. You can't miss trying *quesillo con dulce de alcayota* or *de mamón* or *de miel de caña*.

To accompany your meal, the music at El Sanjuanino is in tune with the regional flavors, and the waiters, as is said about people from the country, never stint on smiles or recommendations.

LA ESQUINA HOMERO MANZI

Café–Restaurante

....

SAN JUAN *3601* ~ BOEDO

☎ *4957.8488*

MONDAY *to* THURSDAY: 6AM *to* 2PM

FRIDAY *and* SATURDAY: 24 HOURS

"**S**AN JUAN Y BOEDO ANTIGUO Y TODO EL CIELO. POMPEYA Y MÁS ALLÁ LA INUNDACIÓN. TU MELENA DE NOVIA EN EL *recuerdo. Y tu nombre flotando en el adiós…*"

The lyrics to one of the most famous tangos, *Sur*, were written on this corner by Homero Manzi when this bar was still called "Cannadian" and was already synonymous with tango, serving as the meeting place for the most famous tango singers. Today, many years later and after an extensive redesign, it still retains its traditional spirit and still honors tango. It was also the gathering place of choice for the writer Roberto Arlt and the political leader Alfredo Palacios.

Today, it can be said that La Esquina Homero Manzi is more of a theme bar and restaurant in the evenings. There are tango shows every day on the big stage at the back of the room, which is decorated with portraits of tango greats painted by Hermenegildo Sabat. There is also a shop where you can purchase T-shirts with images of tango singers, pens, and reproductions of the paintings on the walls.

During the day, it is still a typical Buenos Aires bar. A daily special is offered and is welcomed by tourists and *porteños* alike. *Picadas* and cold cuts in general are of top quality.

RECUERDO - LA ESQUINA DE OSVALDO PUGLIESE

Bar

....

BOEDO *909* ~ BOEDO

☎ *4931~2142*

DAILY: 7AM *to* 2AM

THE CORNER OF BOEDO AND CARLOS CALVO HAS BEEN A POPULAR MEETING PLACE SINCE THE NINETEENTH century. At the beginning, it was a *pulpería* (a kind of inn); later it became a social club; finally, a legendary bar. Its fame was fueled by a pair of regulars—Osvaldo Pugliese, one of the most important tango musicians of all times, and his wife—

who made this bar their regular stopping place on their daily walk from Almagro, where they lived, to Nueva Pompeya.

Rumor has it that tango singer Carlos Gardel used to come here, too, to have a coffee before his performances, sitting next to the window overlooking the street bearing his name. As he gave many performances in a theater half a block away, it is quite possibly true!

Today, this spot has two names. During

the day, it is called Recuerdo, and acts as a busy café still frequented by old tango singers in search of a refreshing drink and dishes like *mondongo a la española*, which is not easily found elsewhere in Buenos Aires.

At night, it is better known as La Esquina de Osvaldo Pugliese, when the audience at paper-topped tables has dinner and shares wine while enjoying a show in which everyone can participate in the singing, just as it used to be in the old days—everyone has some tango soul in Buenos Aires!

ALBAMONTE

Restaurant

. . . .

AV. CORRIENTES 6735 ~ CHACARITA

☎ 4553.2400 / 4554.4486

TUESDAY to SUNDAY: LUNCH and DINNER

CLOSED MONDAYS

THE TRADITION OF GOOD EATING IS INTRINSIC TO BUENOS AIRES AND ITS CITIZENS. NOT EVEN THE WORST CRISIS could erase the custom of eating out. Opened nearly sixty years ago, Albamonte is a real gastronomic gem in the Chacarita neighborhood. Every weekday evening, entire families gather here at big tables topped by white tablecloths and generous breadbaskets as they eagerly await the waiter's recommedations for the evening. Or, they might request tradi-tional dishes that can't be found outside Argentina.

The large room is crammed with tables filled with enthusiastic custom-ers, typical of the style of this classic restaurant, where the walls are covered with photos, and hams hang from the ceiling, leading the way to the kitchen. When you come in for the first time, you have that funny "I've been here before" sensation, the same feeling one experienced in the classic restaurants of mid-twentieth-cen-

tury Buenos Aires, which are quickly disappearing.

Even though dishes are varied, the order of the day here is pizza, with traditional and new flavors. Options for starters are tempting: Parma ham with *ensalada rusa*, sopresatta, *matambre*, and *picada Albamonte*. The main courses—from pasta, fish, and meat to those harder to find like *sesos de novillo a la provezal, riñoncitos a la veneciana, escalopes a la marsala*—ensure it's always crowded. I recommend you book a table before going.

For desserts, there is the specialty of the house, which you really can't miss: *tapa de merengue* (which is cooked overnight in a low oven) with *dulce de leche*, a traditional Argentine delight. Be sure to go to Albamonte hungry, and happy enough to experience a true feast for the senses.

VICENTE

Restaurant

....

PEDRO IGNACIO RIVERA *3801*
(CORNER RÓMULO NAÓN) ~ COGHLAN
☎ *4542.4025*
MONDAY *to* SUNDAY: LUNCH *and* DINNER
CLOSED TUESDAYS

VICENTE IS ONE OF THOSE RESTAURANTS THAT YOU CAN FIND ONLY IF A FOOD LOVER TELLS YOU OF ITS EXISTENCE, or if you are lucky enough to live near one of its four branches.

The first branch opened in the eighties and Vicente gradually expanded with the loyalty of its customers. It is a pleasure to go to a neighborhood like Coghlan and visit a bright cheerful place like this. You can eat good homemade food at reasonable prices here, in a relaxed and unpretentious family atmosphere. The daily specials are the most tempting. The classic starters—a huge variety of original salads, pastas, and risottos—and a mixed grill of meats, which helps one avoid the difficult decision of choosing, explain the success of this family of chefs. The ambiance is friendly and relaxed, especially for those who want to make lunch or dinner a family gathering.

DON CARLOS
Restaurant
. . . .

BRANDSEN *699* (CORNER DEL VALLE IBERLUCEA)

LA BOCA (OPPOSITE BOCA JUNIORS STADIUM)

☎ *4362.2433*

DAILY: LUNCH *through* DINNER

CLOSED SUNDAYS *(and when Boca play at home)*

CASH ONLY

DON CARLOS IS ONLY FOR THOSE WHO KNOW HOW TO MAKE A FEAST OUT OF EATING. STEPPING INTO THIS SMALL restaurant opposite the legendary Boca Stadium means entering Carlos Zinola's house. Therefore, it's "Carlitos" who decides what it is eaten, going from table to table offering small portions of the most varied of dishes, fresh from the kitchen or off the grill, of which only he himself is in charge. Everything is top quality. *Buñuelos* (fritters) and empanadas as starters, then pasta and meat. He won't stop bringing food to your table until you have said you've had enough, and he moves among his customers offering to other diners what wasn't selected by another table. He discovers the taste of his customers just by instinct. Don Carlos is always ready to

talk; he makes you feel like a friend of the house from the moment you sit down.

Players and managers from Boca Juniors, politicians from all branches of government, and lovers of good food make up the usual crowd. And, as Carlos himself likes to boast, his is Francis Ford Coppola's favorite restaurant when the film director is in town.

The neighborhood of La Boca has kept the same spirit since its beginnings: Sheet metal houses, hubbub, colors, the spirit of tango. Some people even believe that Buenos Aires was established just a block from here. Don Carlos is one of the best-kept secrets of the neighborhood. Without exception, you must book, and you must come with time on your hands and be willing to chat. Suddenly, Don Carlos' daughter appears offering desserts. When you say no—because you literally have no more room for dessert—she puts the plate on the table and says, "How come you won't try it, I've just made it myself!"

EL OBRERO
Restaurant
....

AGUSTÍN R. CAFFARENA *64* ~ LA BOCA

☎ *4362.9912*

MONDAY *to* SATURDAY: LUNCH *and* DINNER

CLOSED SUNDAYS *and* PUBLIC HOLIDAYS

EL OBRERO IS IN A SPOT WHERE THE RIVER BECOMES THE HARBOR, NEAR THE STADIUM OF BOCA JUNIORS—ONE of the most beloved football teams in Argentina. It began as a restaurant popular with workers in the area who had to find good, generous and, above all, cheap food, but it gradually became one of the restaurants most frequented by *porteños* who enjoy good barbecued meat. It is without a doubt one of the favorites of those visiting the city, those seeking "the real flavor of Buenos Aires." El Obrero is still loyal to itself and to its fame. The stars of the menu are *asado de tira*, offal, *milanesa* served with french fries, or *rabas*. Their soup comes highly recommended, especially in winter, as does the *berenjenas en escabeche*.

Since it became famous, there has been a notable contrast between the luxury cars parked in front of the restaurant and La Boca's working class character. Yet this juxtaposition is a hallmark of El Obrero, whose main attractions are still its food and the honesty of the presentation.

LA CANCHA

Restaurant

....

BRANSEN *697* ~ LA BOCA

☎ *4362.2975*

DAILY: 10AM *to* 2AM

I N THE HEART OF LA BOCA, IT IS INEVITABLE THAT THE COLORS OF THIS SIMPLE SEAFOOD RESTAURANT ARE BOCA Juniors' blue and yellow. La Cancha resembles the souvenir shop for the team, their stadium being just a few meters away.

Adored by Boca fans and by the locals, La Cancha is also frequented by those who like to experience a true local culinary experience in the neighborhood. La Cancha is the perfect balance between quality and price. Specialists in Spanish cuisine, it is said to have the best seafood in Buenos Aires. You shouldn't miss trying paella or the very tender *rabas* here. Everything is prepared on the spot, even the cream that accompanies homemade flan is beaten the moment you order this dessert.

During the week, there are daily specials. And on Sunday, if you are in a hurry because you must reach *la Bombonera* for the match, you only have to say so and waiters and chefs will hurry to guarantee that you get to the stadium on time.

LA PERLA

Café-Bar-Restaurant

....

PEDRO DE MENDOZA *1899* ~ LA BOCA

☎ *4301.2985*

MONDAY *to* FRIDAY: LUNCH

SATURDAY *and* SUNDAY: LUNCH *and* DINNER

LA PERLA IS LOCATED IN THE TOURIST EPICENTER OF LA BOCA, RIGHT WHERE CALLE CAMINITO BEGINS. OPENED in 1920, it is a café, bar, and restaurant. This bend of Riachuelo is one among many mythical places said to be where Pedro de Mendoza founded Buenos Aires. It was also, at the beginning of the twentieth century, an area full of brothels frequented by sailors in port. These curious facts infuse La Perla with a bit of mystery.

Come here to have a coffee, a drink, and to take advantage of the virtues of a typical canteen which offers a varied menu from *picadas* with beer to the most elaborate Buenos Airean dishes. The doors and the windows are ornamented with the typical art nouveau-like *filetes*, and the walls, covered with old advertising posters, create a nearly cinematic atmosphere. There are tango shows on weekends, since it couldn't be any other way in this city, or in this neighborhood.

CENTRO VASCO FRANCÉS

Restaurant

. . . .

MORENO *1370* ~ MONTSERRAT

☎ *4381.5415*

MONDAY *to* SATURDAY: LUNCH *through* DINNER

SUNDAY: LUNCH

CENTRO VASCO FRANCÉS OPENED IN 1895 AND WAS INTENDED TO BE A MEETING PLACE, OR A KIND OF SOCIAL club, for the French-Basque community of immigrants who came to Buenos Aires with grand hopes and a willingness to work. Among the

traditional activities of the club, only the game of *pelota paleta* (racquet-ball) and the gatherings around good Basque food remain.

The restaurant, open to the general public, is in a former ballroom. Two art deco chandeliers mark the sober and traditional style typical of these places. Superb is the best way to describe the food. There are *setas a la plancha* with garlic, octopus, all types of fish. However, Vasco Francés' sig-

nature dish is *mar y tierra* made with two kinds of rice—one black, rich with squid ink, explains the waiter with pride. Some years ago, Centro Vasco Francés was named one of the four best seafood restaurants in the world, distinguished by its cook, who is from Tucumán, a province in northern Argentina where the sea is merely a mirage. But this is a clear example of how Spanish cuisine has taken root in this country, where the mixture of traditions has become one of its defining strengths.

LA EMBAJADA
Bar-Restaurant
....

SANTIAGO DEL ESTERO 88 ~ MONTSERRAT
☎ 4381.1520
DAILY: 8:30AM to 9PM

AVENIDA DE MAYO AND THE SURROUNDING STREETS ARE THE BASTION OF THE SPANISH COMMUNITY IN BUENOS Aires. It is here that the best restaurants in the Iberian tradition can be found and the distinctive La Embajada is among them. With two entrance doors—one for the bar and the other for the grocery store—it is renowned among office workers in the area thanks to the quality of its hams, stews, and fish. (It is especially important to those who work in the Pasaje Barolo, an architectural gem that was once the highest building in Latin America. Its architect, Mario Palanti, based it on the Divine Comedy and its dome is composed of a lighthouse with 300,000 lamps.)

On Fridays, La Embajada offers its customers *puchero mixto*. It is important to arrive early because the dish has gained such popularity that it is very common for the restaurant to run out by midday. In the afternoon and evening, the original bar, composed of four different kinds of marble, is a meeting point for the regulars who chat and discuss the day's events over sherry.

LA PUERTO RICO

Café

....

ALDOLFO ALSINA *416* ~ MONTSERRAT

☎ *4331.4178*

MONDAY *to* FRIDAY: 7AM *to* 7PM, SATURDAY: 7AM *to* 11AM

THIS CAFÉ, WHICH WAS ORIGINALLY ESTABLISHED ELSE-WHERE IN 1887, SET UP SHOP HERE IN 1925, IN ONE OF the oldest buildings in Buenos Aires. One block from the Colegio Nacional de Buenos Aires, the history of La Puerto Rico is deeply tied to the famous students who met here to study and have impassioned political debates. During the colonial era, the old quarter of the city extended just a few blocks farther than Aldolfo Alsina and this area was full of cafés where people dreamed of and planned the revolution that eventually paved the way for independence.

The star of the house is undoubtedly coffee, accompanied by pastries, fancy biscuits, and cakes, but students are big consumers of sandwiches and the daily specials, so La Puerto Rico now offers quite a varied menu. With marble tables and the usual formal wait sevice, it has been declared a "*sitio de interés cultural y café notable.*" This is one of those places that makes you want to know more about the history of the city and one way of doing so is simply to sit at one of its tables for a while.

LOS TREINTA Y SEIS BILLARES

Bar

....

AV. DE MAYO *1265* ~ MONTSERRAT

☎ *4381.5696*

MONDAY *to* THURSDAY: 8 *to* 3 PM

FRIDAY *and* SATURDAY: 24 HOURS, SUNDAY: 3 *to* 12 PM

L OS 36 BILLARES OPENED IN 1894, THE SAME YEAR AS AVE-NIDA DE MAYO, SO THE HISTORY OF THIS BAR CAN'T BE told without relating it to the most Spanish artery in Buenos Aires. This big avenue was intended to join the presidential residence with the Congress and to give the city a certain European majesty. This is why many Spaniards opened shops along Avenida de Mayo. Set in this context, this bar was born with a certain peculiarity: the billiards tables and the customers' willingness to play. Important chess players made their first moves here and great poets like Federico García Lorca spent their time in Buenos Aires enjoying chats over coffee here. Today it is kept in the same way: that's why it was declared a place of cultural interest for the city together with Café Tortoni and some others. There are shows at night and it operates as a restaurant at lunchtime. Typically *porteño*. Open 24 hours on weekends. You can order coffee all day, that's why this is the home of many who devote their days to the quiet activity of meeting.

PALACIO ESPAÑOL
Restaurant
....

BERNARDO DE IRIGOYEN *180* ~ **MONTSERRAT**

☎ *4334.4876* / *4342.4380*

DAILY: LUNCH *and* DINNER

CLUB ESPAÑOL IS IN ONE OF THE OLDEST BUILDINGS IN THE CENTER OF BUENOS AIRES. BUILT IN 1908 IN THE SPANISH Imperial style, it is an architectural and historical monument. On the ground floor of the building is Palacio Español where passersby have access to the best Iberian food mixed with time honored staples of

Buenos Airean cuisine. The name of the place couldn't be more appropriate since it is impossible not to be taken with the ornamentation and style of the dining room. With just a little bit of imagination, we could be in a room of the Spanish court.

Any dish is a good choice. Starters such as cheese and cold cuts, or

the selection of special salami which can be served with just a torti-lla, are more than filling. If you want to arrange a dinner with friends, the star of the evening might be *cochinillo como en Segovia* (Segovian suckling pig). Beside each table are the traditional tins of red pepper, the perfect accompaniment for any of the dishes offered here. Palacio Español is special for being a quiet place in the middle of the hubbub and for transporting diners back in history.

EL TORTONI

Café

....

AV. DE MAYO *825* ~ MONTSERRAT

☎ *4342.4328*

MONDAY *to* SATURDAY: 8AM *to* 3:30PM

SUNDAY: 8AM *to* 1PM

FOUNDED IN 1858, EL TORTONI IS THE OLDEST AND MOST FAMOUS CAFÉ IN BUENOS AIRES. WHEN IT MOVED A FEW blocks to its present location thirty years after its opening, the entrance was on Calle Rivadavia because Avenida de Mayo, which would join the presidential residence to the Congress in a grand sweep reminiscent of the big Parisian boulevards, hadn't been planned yet. When the first entrance opened, it was the first café to take its tables out to the street, thus establishing a fashion that would later characterize the

big avenue. At that time, personalities from the worlds of culture and politics would have heated discussions about the future of the country at El Tortoni, while they were having a hot chocolate with *churros, leche merengada*, or apéritifs at night. By 1926, the new owner allowed a group of intellectuals to establish "La Peña del Tortoni," a club whose meetings were held in the basement. Important figures such as Juan

de Dios Filiberto, González Tuñón, Alfonsina Storni, Luigi Pirandello, Carlos Gardel, and the famous painter Quinquela Martín, among others, took part in the *peña*.

Today, the café retains the style it adopted in 1888. The furniture is the same: oak marble tables, chairs upholstered in burgundy fabric. In the basement, jazz and tango shows, as well as other activities which add to the café's character, are offered. Regular customers still play chess or billiards in its rooms, like they used to 140 years ago. On the first floor is the National Academy of Tango, where singers, dancers, and poets dazzle on the dance floor every night. El Tortoni is still frequented by politicians who work in the area, lovers of old Buenos Aires, and visitors lured by a bit of history.

Food is the typical café fare, with simple dishes. *Picadas* with draft beer or cider speak to the tradition of the place—there are few places that still observe this custom. *Cortados*, toasted sandwiches, and croissants are an excellent accompaniment to El Tortoni's traditional atmosphere.

EL POBRE LUIS

Steakhouse

....

ARRIBEÑOS *2393* (CORNER BLANCO ENCALADA) ~ NÚÑEZ

☎ *4780.5847* / *4782.4488*

MONDAY *to* SATURDAY: EVENINGS

I N THE NORTHERN NEIGHBORHOOD OF NÚÑEZ, EL POBRE LUIS IS RUN BY ITS OWNER, LUIS ACUÑA, WHO PROVES HIS talent as a host in the traditional sense. He is always at the grill while supervising everything else that is happening in the restaurant; he's alert to dishes going from kitchen to dining room; he stokes the good mood of the waiters; and he also shares the delights of eating well with his chefs. He is even in charge of decorating the place; like an old local grocery, it is fitted out with the traditional football jerseys, pictures, and pennants.

El Pobre is a family restaurant frequented by the residents of Núñez and other parts of the city—especially those who come to see the River Plate football team on weekends; their stadium is nearby.

With excellent barbecued meat and delicious sweet potatoes with honey, the sophistication of which can surprise the unprepared customer, El Pobre Luis is also famous for its delicious *pamplonas*, always ready for those who want to savor a different taste of the typical Buenos Aires *parrilla*.

ANGELÍN
Pizzeria
....

AV. CÓRDOBA *5270* ~ PALERMO / VILLA CRESPO

☎ *4774.3836*

DAILY: 6PM *to* MIDNIGHT

═══════════════════════════════════════

RADITION HAS MADE SOME PLACES SACROSANCT; PLACES THAT ARE PART OF THE HISTORY OF BUENOS AIRES AND its people. Angelín Pizzeria exemplifies this. It was founded in 1905 on Avenida Córdoba bordering the trendy Palermo Viejo neighborhood, where the Maldonado Canal was the boundary of the city—and of decency—toward the end of the nineteenth century. A poster inside states that they are the creators of *pizza canchera*, a huge cheeseless pizza meant to be shared among friends after football matches. When the football matches are broadcast on television, Angelín is as crowded as ever.

The place is bustling, full of men, and almost gloomy, but its pizzas and empanadas transcend the fashionable trends of the area. *Porteños* enjoy eating at the bar overlooking the street. The famous trio "moscato, pizza, y faina" find their *raison d'etre* here.

Empanadas, *fainá*, *fugazas*, and *fugazzetas* are the favorites among grandfathers, sons, and grandsons who make this their hangout. Many of them have left the neighborhood, but come back in search of the unmistakable taste and the irreplaceable owner.

BAR DEL GALLEGO
Café–Restaurant
....

BONPLAND *1703* ~ PALERMO HOLLYWOOD

☎ *4771.1526*

MONDAY *to* FRIDAY: 6AM *to* 10PM

SATURDAY: 6AM *to* 8PM

WHERE THE PALERMO NEIGHBORHOOD IS NOW CALLED HOLLYWOOD, A FEW METERS FROM THE AMERICA TV headquarters and the Metro 95.1 radio station, sits Bar del Gallego, which remains somewhat incongrous in the trendy dining scene surrounding it. At lunchtime there are special dishes, all of which are good and are served in generous portions. In the afternoon and evening, sandwiches are the main players, especially the Parma ham, which is personally cut by *el Gallego* himself while he mumbles something incomprehensible. This is the place where neighborhood office workers stop by for lunch and where old-timers mix with recently arrived actors and journalists. Bar del Gallego closes early, so it is ideal for breakfast, lunch, and meetings in the mid-afternoon. It is perfect for those looking for an unpretentious place for a casual meeting or for those who like reading and relaxing in an old-fashioned place where time seems to have its own pace.

CLUB EROS

Restaurant

....

URIARTE *1609* ~ PALERMO VIEJO

☎ *4832.1313*

DAILY: LUNCH *through* DINNER

CLUB EROS IS AT THE INTERSECTION OF HONDURAS AND URIARTE, RIGHT IN THE HEART OF GLAMOROUS AND fashionable Palermo Soho. It is a local club like many others that have vanished in the area, and it has the charm of being unique and eternal.

Past the reception area—a patio where tables are placed on busy weekends—are doors to the dining room, where the friendly waiters recite the night's dishes. There is no written menu, but there certainly is a guarantee that everything served at Club Eros is typical of Buenos Aires: simple and of top quality. There is usually roast beef, salads, and homemade pasta. Sparkling water comes to your table in old-fashioned siphon bottles.

El Eros, as regular customers usually call it, is always crowded with locals and those who enjoy strolling around Palermo's beautiful streets. Everyone is eating well, at accessible prices, in a place where you're made to feel at home. Popular with groups, it is common to see people waiting to get a table on weekends. Tables can be booked only if you are a regular customer or a very good friend of the house.

DON JULIO
Restaurant — Steakhouse

....

GUATEMALA *4691* (CORNER GURRUCHAGA) ~ PALERMO
☎ *4831.9564* / *4832.6058*
DAILY: LUNCH *through* DINNER

DON JULIO IS A LOCAL RESTAURANT WITH THE FLAVORS OF THE CLASSIC *PARRILLAS*, OR GRILL RESTAURANTS, AND the friendliness of the ones that have managed to endure through the years. Surviving in the most fashionable neighborhood in Buenos Aires, Don Julio is a tribute to the Argentine spirit.

The traditional starters, *parrillada*, *asado*, offal, and even pasta are honest, simple dishes. An excellent wine list is accompanied by the waiter's suggestions. The dining room is decorated with typical items from the countryside—leather pieces, and objects associated with the *gauchos*—but the best place to eat is outside, sheltered under the shadow of the trees on this still-cobbled street. Even though the old neighborhood has been taken over by the latest trends in design and fashion, you

can still detect the aroma of spring, just as in decades past, when there was a winery down the street from Don Julio and the locals were drinking *mate* on the sidewalk, watching the day go by.

EL PREFERIDO DE PALERMO

Restaurant

....

JORGE LUIS BORGES *2108* ~ PALERMO

☎ *4774.6585*

MONDAY *to* SATURDAY: LUNCH *and* DINNER

SUNDAY: LUNCH

E L PREFERIDO DE PALERMO IS OPPOSITE THE SPOT—THE CORNER OF GUATEMALA AND SERRANO—IMMORTALIZED by Jorge Luis Borges in his poem *Buenos Aires*, as the "mythical foundation" of the city (and very near the Borges family home, marked by a plaque, but not much else).

El Preferido is a restaurant and an old-style local grocer. Familiarity, kindness, and professionalism merge in this bastion of tradition located in what now might be the chicest neighborhood in the city. You can eat at tableclothed tables in the restaurant, which used to be the patio of this old house, or at the high tables in the grocery, where you can have sandwiches made with the best Parma ham or one of the daily specials: lentils, tripe, *puchero*, *fabada Asturiana*. Everything is tempting.

The best way to describe this steeped-in-history treasure is by listing some of the dishes. The vast menu offers *vithel thoné*, *revuelto gramajo*, tortillas, octopus, Spanish sardines, *pejerrey Gran Paraná*, kidneys in sherry sauce, *bife de costilla* (T-bone steak). It is impossible to make a

quick decision, but luckily there's no hurry at El Preferido. While you look at the menu, you can savor the pâté of the day with a glass of sherry. And you'll leave feeling sated and happy, filled with the spirit of the ambiance of the place, and of the presence of Borges, who wrote: "Hard to believe Buenos Aires had any beginning. / I feel it to be as eternal as air and water."

We recommend: everything.

GASCÓN
Restaurant
....

AV. CÓRDOBA *3999* ~ PALERMO
☎ *4862.9662*
DAILY: NOON *to* 4AM

═══════════════════════════════

GASCÓN, AS IF PART OF ITS DESTINY, IS AT A KEY CROSS-ING OF AVENUES AND NEIGHBORHOODS, AND IT IS THE preference of middle class *porteños*, who have always known that it is possible to eat well, yet inexpensively.

Gascón has a typically homey fifties style: lots of tables, hanging hams, shelves heaving with wine bottles, a kitchen in view of the dining room, and big glass windows to watch and be watched by those walking toward the heart of Palermo.

Grilled meat is excellent and served in generous portions—"*Hay lechón*" (Pork is served) announces the sign next to the entrance. Many daily specials seem to pay homage to Spanish conquerors and civil servants of the old vice-royalty of the River Plate: from the classic *papas españolas* to *chipirones rellenos* (small stuffed cuttlefish), not to mention *bacalao a la vizcaína* (a cod and vegetable dish).

Itself a blend of neighborhoods and traditional cuisines, Gascón shows that mixtures are possible and successful. Gascón is always here, untouched by fashion, always ready to be rediscovered.

GUIDO'S BAR
Restaurant
. . . .
REPÚBLICA DE LA INDIA *2843* ~ PALERMO

☎ *4802.2391*

MONDAY *to* FRIDAY: 7AM *to* 2AM

SATURDAY: 7AM *to* 4PM

THE SMALL AND LIVELY GUIDO'S BAR IS OPPOSITE THE BOTANICAL GARDENS. IT SEEMS TO HAVE BEEN LIFTED intact from an exquisite village in Tuscany and dropped in the middle of one of the most beautiful streets in Buenos Aires.

Entering Guido's means being ready to step somewhat into the unknown. Without a menu and with no fixed prices, Carlos, the owner, chooses your menu himself and takes dishes to your table as you try them out. A selection of hors d'oeuvre, pasta, tapas, and homemade pizza are only some of the excellent dishes you shouldn't miss. This is the game at Guido's and therein lies its mystery. Relax in the warm welcome and enjoy this gastronomic oasis without thinking much about the bill. If you like eating well, you will be more than happy here.

With checked tablecloths and the walls papered with maps and photographs of the Marx Brothers, Albert Einstein, the Argentine comedian Alberto Olmedo, Andy Warhol, and John Lennon, Guido's is a simple, but at the same time, sophisticated restaurant, where lemon mousse and tiramisu are essential to ending a good night.

HERMANN
Restaurant
....
AV. SANTA FÉ *3902* ~ PALERMO

☎ *4832.1929*

DAILY: NOON *to* 4PM *and* 8PM *to* 1:30AM

THIS OLD RESTAURANT, OPPOSITE THE BOTANICAL GARDENS, WAS FAMOUS AS A GERMAN BEER HALL when it opened, but it did not take long before it turned into the most popular restaurant in the area thanks to a combination of excellent food and reasonable prices. The decor, in strict German style, is highlighted by posters of famous Bavarian castles and by the aluminum-topped bar where draught beer is poured. Besides, there are still those classic booths that give Hermann that unique touch of secrecy and intimacy. It is also well-known for the friendliness of its waiters, most of whom have been working here for thirty years or more and who always have the right suggestion to make your choice of dishes more enjoyable (and sometimes

more suitable): sausages with sauerkraut, *milanesas*, salads, and the unbeatable *suprema Maryland*, an Argentine invention with a foreign name.

The small room and outsized reputation can sometimes keep you waiting for a free table. In the meantime, you can have an apéritif at the bar while looking at those diners in the big mirror who will surrender their seat for you in no time at all.

LA CASA POLACA
Restaurant
....

JORGE LUIS BORGES *2076* ~ PALERMO

☎ *4899.0514*

TUESDAY *to* **SATURDAY: DINNER**

ALL THE IMMIGRANT COMMUNITIES THAT ARRIVED IN BUENOS AIRES AT THE BEGINNING OF THE TWENTIETH century created social clubs where they could meet their compatriots and not lose touch with the roots, memories, and flavors of their homeland. This is how La Casa Polaca was born, an old building reminiscent of central Europe right in the heart of Palermo Viejo.

Around twenty-five years ago, Antos, a chef who was educated in France, and the son of Polish immigrants, arrived and gave this basement the liveliness and magic that has made La Casa Polaca a cult restaurant here. Until 1990, it was only open to members or by special invitation, and like a secret club, one must go downstairs to access the warm dining room for *barszcz* (beet soup), *sledz* (herring marinated in cream), pierogi ruskie, or goulash delight. It isn't just Polish and Jewish Argentines who enjoy the menu here, but anyone who finds a taste of home in traditional Central European cuisine.

DOM POLSKI

ÑA SERAPIA

Home Cooking

. . . .

AV LAS HERAS *3357* ~ PALERMO

☎ *4801.5307*

DAILY: NOON *to* 4PM *and* 7PM *to* MIDNIGHT

TO PARAPHRASE EDGAR ALLAN POE'S CLASSIC TALE, *THE PUR-LOINED LETTER*: THE SOLUTION TO A MYSTERY IS USUALLY in sight. That is the case at Ña Serapia, a well-kept secret located opposite Parque Las Heras, within everyone's sight, but known by few and feverishly adored by those who do.

Like every legendary place, its fame spreads by word of mouth and its charm lies in its authenticity, which has persisted over the years and weathered changing times and fashions. Ña Serapia is a small regional restaurant. Its specialties are typical dishes from the north of Argentina like *locro, humitas en tamales*, and the truly unmissable *quesillo de cabra con miel* for dessert.

On Avenida Las Heras, which was called Calle del Chavango at the beginning of the twentieth century and was the northern access route out of the city, Ña Serapia has a very small, simple dining room, which makes it cozy and always popular. Discovering Ña Serapia and tasting everything offered is undoubtedly to find an Argentine treasure in the heart of the city.

PUNTO Y BANCA

Pizzeria

. . . .

HONDURAS *4002* ~ PALERMO

☎ *4864.4268*

DAILY: 11AM *to* 1AM

ANYONE WHO COMES INTO THIS TINY PIZZERIA KNOWS THEY ARE REALLY GOING TO A PARTY. HERE, ON THIS corner between Palermo and Almagro, the master pizza makers, the owner, and the waiters cheerfully celebrate lunchtime. It's noisy and full of taxi drivers, but at heart it is basically a pizzeria where you eat standing at the bar, the way all good pizza should be eaten.

Fugazzeta rellena, traditional mozzarella, fried empanadas, all the options will lead to indulging in more than just one portion, while the television blares the news and suited men undo their ties to feel more like the locals.

There are many places like this in Buenos Aires; however, they're difficult to find. They are only known by word of mouth and loyalty is expected by the owners. Don't panic if the corner is crowded; many are having a quick snack or waiting for a pizza to go. Persevere and you'll be rewarded.

VARELA VARELITA
Café

. . . .

SCALABRINI ORTIZ *and* PARAGUAY ~ PALERMO

NO PHONE

DAILY: 7AM *to* 9PM

ON THE CORNER OF SCALABRINI ORTIZ AND PARAGUAY BORDERING PALERMO SOHO, A NEIGHBORHOOD WHERE everything has been recycled, the original Varela Varelita still lives on. What was once a liquor store more than forty years ago is now a café frequented by passersby, students from the area, and loyal regular customers who are looking for an old-fashioned place, far from the rage

of trends. In the nineties, Varela Varelita rose to fame because of the politicians who breakfasted there and the journalists who waited for their first statements of the day.

With no regular menu, the waiter lists the typical options: coffees, sandwiches, and milkshakes. It's very important to nurture your relationship with a waiter in bars like Varela Varelita. Not only is what's offered to you dependent on him, but also what he brings you with your order: the exact amount of milk, the best croissants available, the sandwich with the crunchiest bread.

The tables, like in nearly all the local bars and cafés, are mostly taken by men who sit alone with the papers (offered at the café or bought from the newsstand at the entrance), or who chat with each other, forming a sort of brotherhood of men who sit alone. The favorite tables, of course, are those next to the big windows—perfect for people watching, and the table hidden behind the only column in the room, ideal for secret meetings which, with the complicity of the waiter, will be kept as such.

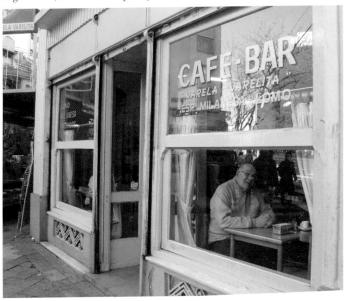

LAS VIOLETAS

Restaurant-Bar

. . . .

USPALLATA *2801* (CORNER LABARDÉN) ~ PARQUE PATRICIOS

☎ *4911.1993*

MONDAY *to* FRIDAY: 8AM *to* 7PM

ON AN ORDINARY CORNER IN PARQUE PATRICIOS, WHERE YOU DON'T EXPECT TO BE SURPRISED BY ANYTHING, it is precisely the ordinariness which gives value to this bar/restaurant/hangout. Stepping into Las Violetas is to go back in time, or put another way, to enter a timeless space — a place where what is important is the leisure time, the chats, and the friendly rapport with the owner, who takes bread and butter to your table at breakfast with the same enthusiasm as he does a lentil stew or a generous portion of the best Parma ham at dinner.

Las Violetas, a few blocks from Huracán football stadium, awakens loyalty like very few other places; doctors from the nearby hospital, area office workers, and old neighbors always return. Lately, it has become the norm to see the bar used as a film set stand-in for old Buenos Aires, the Buenos Aires in many people's hearts which tends to disappear if it's not properly looked after. Las Violetas means homemade food and comfort, tradition, and memories. It is a special place for intimate talks and for moments of introspection.

EL BALÓN

Bar — Restaurant

. . . .

GAONA 3199 ~ LA PÂTERNAL

☎ 4581.4626

DAILY: BREAKFAST *through* DINNER

EL BALÓN TAKES UP A CORNER IN THE HEART OF LA PÂTÉRNAL. IT IS THE KIND OF PLACE WHERE MEN FOND OF long conversation converge and compete with the sound from the television in the background. It is run by an owner who, most of the time, is in charge of seeing to the quality of the food and to the different tastes of his customers. The waiters have been working here for about thirty years and it shows; they are the kings of the room. Neighbors come here to chat at snack time. They'll drink draft beer in summer in front of the large windows open to Calle Bolivia. El Balón is a typical neighborhood bar, where even those who have moved away come back to visit. Some people can't help coming in when they walk past, even if just to have a drink at the bar, or when tempted by the kitchen's good sausages and french fries. El Balón is the ideal place to start the day before going to work or to take a break and relax before heading home.

CARRITOS DE LA COS-TANERA SUR

Steakhouse

....

COSTANERA SUR JETTY ~ PUERTO MADERO
ENTRANCE THROUGH PUERTO MADERO
NO PHONE
DAILY: LUNCH *through* DINNER

TWO TYPICALLY BUENOS AIREAN TRADITIONS INTERSECT HERE. NEARLY A HUNDRED YEARS AGO THIS WAS A public beach, used as a promenade by everyone in the city. In summer, people bathed in the river (men and women were scheduled at different times, of course) and in winter, they walked along the water-

front and had tea in the *confectioners*. Early on in the Costanera Norte, there were also concession stands with grills where one could have a quick bite; these later turned into large restaurants that served some of the best authentic Argentine food. The stands, however, remained a tradition thanks to their excellent prices and high quality.

Eventually, the stands disappeared from Costanera Norte, but have been established again at Costanera Sur. Although it is no longer a beach (and you can hardly see the river), it is one of the most popular tourist spots in the city, and here you can find the best steak and *vacío* sandwiches, prepared on the spot on the smoky grill. You can't miss *bondiola* (pork) sandwiches and, of course, *choripán*, one of the most typical foods in the country. Eating these crunchy sandwiches at the waterfront on a sunny day is as deeply rooted an experience of Buenos Aires as seeing tango.

LA BARRA
Restaurant
....

AV LIBERTADOR *932* (CORNER CALLAO) ~ RECOLETA

☎ *4812.1745*

DAILY: 7:30AM *to* 2AM

I N A NEIGHBORHOOD WHERE YOU WOULD EXPECT TO FIND ONLY THE HEIGHT OF SOPHISTICATION AND LUXURY, LA Barra, a popular traditional restaurant, has snuck itself in.

With tablecloths typical of *bodegones* and the homemade dishes of Argentine tradition, La Barra welcomes both locals familiar with the place and the unsuspecting visitor. The welcoming basket of always crunchy bread is just a hint of what is to come; homemade meat roulade, baked chicken with potatoes, steak with french fries, *milanesas*, and pasta, will make you feel as if you're at a family gathering. With windows over-looking the arcades of Avenida Libertador, you can relax in the calm open view of trees, the rumbling train yard, and the river.

Nearly two decades ago, just a few meters from La Barra, one could still see ItalPark, an amusement park which has since disappeared with the restoration of the neighborhood, and which symbolizes, at least for those *porteños* over thirty, a mythical place in the city. Perhaps La Barra had its golden age then, when after a ride on the *Tren Fantasma* (ghost train) or the *Autitos Chocadores* (bumper cars), a family meal would be enjoyed before returning home.

LA COCINA

Home Cooking

....

AV. PUEYRREDÓN *1508* ~ RECOLETA

☎ *4825.3171*

DAILY: 11AM *to* 3PM *and* 6PM *to* MIDNIGHT

I N A SMALL COZY SPOT BETWEEN RECOLETA AND BARRIO NORTE LIES A CENTER OF GREATNESS FOR ARGENTINE FOOD. La Cocina offers the *catamarqueña* version (from Catamarca, a province in the northwest of Argentina) of empanadas, *locro*, tamales, and local desserts.

Customers mix at the bar since there are no tables at La Cocina, which is ideal for a quick stop at midday, or for a unusual dinner, when the charm of regional flavors stands out.

It is said that the best dough in the country for preparing empanadas is made here. The most popular and famous are stuffed with spicy meat and sweet corn, and the *picachu*, stuffed with onion, cheese, and pepper. *Locro* with melted cheese—as it is traditional in Catamarca—is served in a typical clay casserole dish and is always accompanied by the round biscuits served instead of bread in the provinces.

Knowing about La Cocina means knowing a secret. You can always come back at any time of the day to satisfy a whim.

EL RINCÓN
Restaurant
. . . .

URIBURU *1759* ~ RECOLETA

☎ *4803.8273*

MONDAY *to* SATURDAY: NOON *to* 3PM *and* 8PM *to* MIDNIGHT

THE RECOLETA WAS ESTABLISHED BY THE RECOLETOS PRIESTS WHOSE CHURCH, IGLESIA DEL PILAR, STILL STANDS nearby, but by the end of the twentieth century it had become one of the most exclusive and Frenchified areas of Buenos Aires. A block from the most famous cemetery in the city and surrounded by the most refined restaurants, El Rincón (used as the setting for a number of Argentine films of the seventies and eighties, many starring legendary Argentine comedian Alberto Olmedo) still survives, serving a mixture of popular cuisines. If you want to eat generous portions of food that doesn't

have any gastronomic pretensions, this is the place. Tomatoes stuffed with tuna, *costillitas de cerdo a la riojana*, and *matambre con ensalada rusa* are waiting: fresh and ready, just as they have been for more than thirty years.

The longtime owner shows us the wonderful meal being prepared for him and his employees and says, "If we eat this well, imagine how well our customers eat!" There's *paella, rabas, mondongo*, hake, lentils. Today the same style remains: simple and generous portions of Argentine and Spanish dishes, two cuisines that are fused in Buenos Aires.

Unintentionally, the place is almost minimalist in style, with dim lighting and pale walls. The style is simple, old, without special care; hence, authentic and sincere. In the heart of Recoleta, Buenos Aires keeps on beating.

RODI-BAR

Restaurant-Bar

....

VICENTE LÓPEZ *1900* (CORNER AYACUCHO) ~ RECOLETA

☎ *4801.5230*

MONDAY *to* SATURDAY: 6AM *to* 2AM

FINDING A LOCAL BODEGÓN THAT MIXES SPANISH AND ARGEN-TINE FOOD IS NOT COMMON IN THE RECOLETA. HOWEVER, Rodi embodies tradition and popularity in the middle of this neighborhood's novelty and exclusivity. The charm of this place lies in the small cramped tables, the accessible prices, and the waiters in white who are so serious that they actually become rather likable.

Near the cinema complex, Rodi is frequented by those who like eating well without paying extra for eating in such an expensive part of town. Dishes are generously portioned and range from the simple *peceto al horno con papas* (a type of meat that is baked and served with potatoes) to rabbit in white wine. Rodi offers a different menu every day, which is enjoyed by local office workers and by regular customers who stay after lunch to have coffee and people-watch through the sidewalk windows.

EL CUARTITO

Pizzeria

· · · · · · · · · · · · · · · ·

TALCAHUANO *937* ~ RETIRO

☎ *4816.1758 / 4331*

SUNDAY *to* THURSDAY: 11AM *to* 1AM

FRIDAY *and* SATURDAY: 11AM *to* 2AM

YOU CAN'T SAY THAT YOU REALLY KNOW BUENOS AIRES UNTIL YOU'VE EATEN AT EL CUARTITO, SO FAMOUS A SYMBOL of the city that football legend Maradona chose to dine on their pizza following his wedding.

It always ranks among the top choices in the heated discussions about the best pizza in Buenos Aires, but it undoubtedly wins when ambiance comes into play. Full of photographs and posters of famous boxers and football teams and framed jerseys, El Cuartito is an unmissable experience for any visitor to Buenos Aires.

Pizza comes accompanied by the typical glass of Muscatel or a large bottle of beer. El Cuartito's *fainá* (made from chickpea flour, and a near-cousin of Ligurian *farinata*) is by far the star of the menu here and is *the* choice of accompaniment to any meal. Everyone who comes to El Cuartito comes back. And they bring friends and they recommend it to others. Prices are very reasonable and only cash is accepted. Many people succumb to the temptation of stopping by for a bite at the bar before getting on with the rest of their day—only now with a little of Buenos Aires in their hearts.

EL ESTABLO

Restaurant

....

PARAGUAY 489 ~ RETIRO
☎ 4311.1639
DAILY: NOON *to* 2AM

EL ESTABLO HAS TWO ENTRANCES AND EACH LEADS TO A COMPLETELY DIFFERENT PLACE. THE FIRST ENTRANCE, THE most visible, takes us into a typical Buenos Aires bar. The second one, a few meters away, on Calle Paraguay, is the entrance to a surprising place—an authentic Argentine *parrilla*. It is said that the best *bife de chorizo* can be eaten here. All the meat choices are excellent and

prepared to order. But El Establo also offers other unmissable dishes: huge tortillas, *fabada Asturiana*, and *puchero* every Friday. Servings are large and can be easily shared; alternately, you can request half-portions of almost all dishes.

The place is small and has a well-preserved, old-fashioned style. The grill, as well as the hams and the big iron lamps, can be seen from the street. Visited and loved by Argentines and tourists alike, El Establo is

---

located near the old Paseo de Julio—now called Avenida Alem—from where there are wonderful views of the harbor, the old customs buildings, and other symbols of Buenos Aires' port city past; from here Buenos Aires' once significant connection to the rest of world is still resonant.

FLORIDA GARDEN

Café

....

FLORIDA *899* ~ RETIRO

☏ *4312.7902*

MONDAY *to* FRIDAY: 6:30AM *to* MIDNIGHT

SATURDAY: 6:30AM *to* 11PM, SUNDAY: 7:30AM *to* 10PM

IF SOMEBODY HAS A MEETING AT FLORIDA GARDEN, YOU CAN BE SURE THAT IT'S AN IMPORTANT ENGAGEMENT. "THE identity of a corner," reads the slogan on the door at the corner of the pedestrianized Calle Florida and Calle Paraguay. Politicians, businessmen, and artists mark the rhythm of time here. Having a coffee standing at one of the two bars is typical of those preferring a quick

face-to-face chat or the trust of the waiter who serves coffee while he comments on the news of the day.

From the outside, the imposing staircase, part of Florida's uniqueness, is visible through the large windows. Florida Garden is a must-do for those who are fond of good sandwiches, since the specialty of the house is *pebete de pan negro*, a house-baked brown bread roll with ham and cheese or turkey and tomato. *Cuba libre*, as well as whiskey, are the choices here at the end of the day, when men prefer to relax at the bar at the back of the room, putting their work days behind them before escaping from the city center.

The white-aproned and bow-tied waiters, who live up to the tradition of the house, know their clientele very well. They know what to offer, they know about discretion, and they are great secret-keepers. Florida Garden is one of the most traditional, and at the same time rebellious, spots in the city. Famous since the 1960s, this was the gathering place for artists from the famous Di Tella Institute, birthplace of local artistic vanguards. Even today, thanks to its peculiar charm and the elegant neighborhood, different ideologies, classes, and styles still intersect here.

LOS CHILENOS

Restaurant

. . . .

SUIPACHA *1024* ~ RETIRO

☎ *4328.3123*

MONDAY *to* SATURDAY: 11:30AM *to* 4:30PM *and* 7:30PM *to* 1AM

FAR FROM THE ANDES MOUNTAINS, BUT VERY NEAR SOME OF THE MOST IMPORTANT SPOTS IN THE CITY, LOS CHILENOS is a restaurant which serves only Chilean food for cosmopolitan Buenos Aireans who take advantage of the city's eateries as a patchwork of international gastronomic trends.

Within walking distance of the Plaza San Martín and the ever-growing number of art galleries, Los Chilenos shouldn't be missed on any walk around the Retiro. Regional food of excellent quality is expertly prepared—don't pass up any seafood or fish dish, so typical of Chile and so difficult to get in Buenos Aires. *Caldillo de congrio* (conger chowder) will inevitably remind diners of Pablo Neruda and his unforgettable ode to the dish. The ambiance is simple and relaxed in this small unpretentious restaurant. Los Chilenos surprises us with its fresh and comforting flavors in a place where everything otherwise seems so typical of Buenos Aires.

SAINT MORITZ

Bar

....

PARAGUAY *802* (CORNER ESMERALDA) ~ RETIRO

☎ *4311.7311*

MONDAY *to* FRIDAY: 7AM *to* 8PM

SATURDAY: MORNINGS

SAINT MORITZ LOOKS LIKE THE CAFÉ IN A BIG RAILWAY STATION IN EARLY TWENTIETH-CENTURY EASTERN Europe: stuck in time. For more than fifty years, it has insisted on being the perfect place to pass the time. There's a luxurious, masculine atmosphere to the place, but Saint Moritz welcomes loyal regular customers, casual passersby, intellectuals lured by the quietness of the room and the big windows, too.

A few blocks from crowded Florida, a few meters from Plaza San Martín, it doesn't reflect the bustling nature of the area. Its calm, untouchable uniqueness is what makes it everlasting. Being just a simple café is its strong point; it offers toasted sandwiches, breakfast, different kinds of coffee, and spirits. It attracts visitors with whiskey, cognac, and beer in the late afternoon. On weekends it attracts those who come from the outskirts for a walk around the city center, the Recoleta, or Retiro; they come for the hot chocolate with *churros* or a banana milkshake, and afterwards leave stealthily in order to take that imaginary train again, back to oblivion.

ARTURITO
Restaurant
. . . .

AV. CORRIENTES *1124* ~ SAN NICOLÁS

☎ *4382.0227 / 1428*

DAILY: 11AM *to* 4PM *and* 7PM *to* 2AM

ARTURITO IS JUST A FEW METERS FROM EL OBELISCO, THE MONUMENT COMMEMORATING THE 400TH ANNIVERSARY of Buenos Aires. It was erected in 1936 under the direction of architect Alberto Prebisch, one of the main proponents of Argentine modernism. The intersection of Corrientes and 9 de Julio is the heart of the city, where offices and theaters, daytime and nighttime activities coexist with the same intensity.

Arturito, opened in 1904, is an indisputable landmark where you can enjoy rarities like frogs in Provençal sauce, made with garlic and parsley, or stick to a classic like *bife de chorizo*. Behind the white curtains separating diners from Avenida Corrientes, the cheerful environment and din of the place make Arturito the perfect place for large parties rather than a romantic date. But all the dishes share the same high quality and reasonable prices, which go hand in hand with the friendly service of the white-jacketed waiters, always on hand to give you a recommendation or to caution overly enthusiastic customers who, faced with the variety of choices, order too much.

BANCHERO
Pizzeria
....

AV. CORRIENTES *1300* (CORNER TALCAHUANO) ~ SAN NICOLÁS

☎ *4382.3353 / 4669*

MONDAY *to* SATURDAY: 7AM *to* 2AM

SUNDAY: NOON *to* 2AM

BANCHERO IS TYPICAL OF ONE OF BUENOS AIRES' TRA-DITIONAL PIZZERIAS: ALWAYS CROWDED, NOISY WITH waiters hurriedly rushing between tables and negotiating a crowd of friends toasting each other with beer glasses. Of indisputable quality, the pizza is also served by the slice and can be eaten at the bar, which is ideal when you're in a hurry or for satisfying a craving at any time of day. Quite apart from the wide variety of pizza, Banchero is also the original home of the famous *fugazza con queso*.

During the day, Banchero is the setting for groups of office workers chatting over lunch, while at night it is crowded after the end of theater performances or films in the nearby cinemas. It is common knowledge that in order to nab a table at Banchero, you must leave the theater immediately after the performance; this way you will be able to relax in the dining room where opinions about the various shows circulate, friends laugh, and more than one first date has been witnessed—since it is widely known that eating a pizza here is an easy proposal that never fails.

CONFITERÍA IDEAL
Café-Bar

....

SUIPACHA 380 ~ SAN NICOLÁS

☎ 5265.8078

MONDAY to SUNDAY: 8AM to MIDNIGHT

THERE ARE SOME PEOPLE WHO SAY THAT WHEN CAFÉS WERE UPGRADED, THEY WERE CALLED *CONFECTIONERS* (A WORD shared with the places where pastries and cakes are sold). But La Ideal was born in 1912 with a touch of the Parisian tearoom about it, within walking distance of one of the most historic corners in the city: Corrientes and Suipacha. Together with El Tortoni (see page 56) and Confectioner Las Violetas (see page 14), this is one of the oldest and most traditional establishments in Buenos Aires. A treasure of the belle époque, it has just barely adjusted to modern times without losing its style or unique character. The huge room is decorated with stained glass, chandeliers, marble staircases, and the famous pergola that the waiters show off with pride, creating a European atmosphere which at once contrasts with and feeds the spirit of the place, so typical of Buenos Aires.

The spirit of tango prevails here and from 3pm on you can listen to tango beats coming from the second floor, where there is a ballroom, overseen by the most famous *milongueros* in the city and visited by those eager to take lessons.

In its glory days, La Ideal was a meeting place for politicians and men of letters, like many cafés near Avenida Corrientes. Today, it offers

that traditional and somewhat decadent atmosphere reminiscent of Ettore Scola's film *Le Bal*.

From morning until late at night, you can have national and international cuisine for breakfast, lunch, and dinner. Turkey sandwiches, hot chocolate with *churros*, and apéritifs can be ordered without doubt about quality. On Sundays, as usual, it becomes one of the most visited tearooms in the city, where women of all generations dress up for the occasion and waiters bring out the old china.

EL GATO NEGRO

Café

....

AV. CORRIENTES *1669* ~ SAN NICOLÁS

☎ *4374.1730* / *4371.6942*

MONDAY *to* FRIDAY: NOON *through* DINNER.

FRIDAY *and* SATURDAY: EVENINGS *through* DINNER

CLOSED SUNDAYS

LIKE THE SPICE SHOP IT ONCE WAS, ONE WHICH THE MODERN AGE SEEMS TO HAVE FORGOTTEN, EL GATO Negro is a place defined by its aromas. The moment you cross the threshold, the smell of mingling spices mixed with tea leaves and freshly ground coffee envelops you. It opened in 1927 when Avenida Corrientes was still a narrow street, but was already beginning to reveal its destiny as the center of nightlife in Buenos Aires. A few years ago, some tables and Thonet chairs were added so patrons could sample their coffee and tea in an ambiance that is one part Vienna, one part Argentine countryside.

There is a choice of pastries, cakes, and brownies to accompany the beverages, which are the specialty of the house. A bistro has recently opened

on the second floor for those who want a more complete menu, one renowned for its use of exotic spices.

El Gato Negro is one of those places that make Buenos Aires what it is, and that's why it was declared a Café Notable—recognized for its historical significance—so that it can continue beautifying the area, famous for its cinemas and bookshops, with its flavors and its aromas.

EL NAVEGANTE
Restaurant

....

VIAMONTE *158* ~ SAN NICOLÁS

☎ *4311.0641*

MONDAY *to* FRIDAY: 8AM *to* 2AM

SATURDAY: 8AM *to* 3:30PM *and* 7PM *to* MIDNIGHT

LEGENDARY BOXING STADIUM LUNA PARK IS UNQUES-
TIONABLY *THE* INFLUENCING FACTOR THAT ADDS TO THE
style and history of the San Nicolás area. Luna Park is where
notable international fights have taken place and today is home to the
biggest traveling productions and musical performances. El Navegante
is just a few meters from here. Very few notice that it is actually the bar
and restaurant of a hotel long forgotten by both the modern age and
any discernible clientele. But El Navegante has a life of its own. The
word to describe it is *bodegón*—or a little tavern—where customers call
waiters by their first names and take their recommendations for the daily
specials.

The place looks neglected—in keeping with the style—which contrasts greatly with the more sophisticated restaurants in the area. Perhaps
this is one of the reasons for its success. And the food is classic: tortilla,
casserole, *conejito a la cazadora*, and the unmissable *parrilla*. Boxers,
businessmen, and artists have made this traditional restaurant fashionable again. Those who come here are looking for something legendary
and for a feast of good Argentine food.

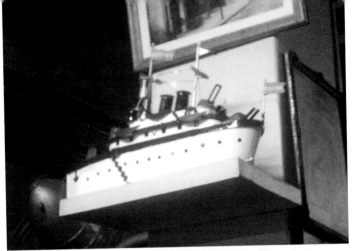

EL PALACIO DE LA PAPA FRITA

Restaurant

....

AV. CORRIENTES *1612* ~ SAN NICOLÁS

☎ *4374.8073 / 0920*

DAILY: NOON *to* 2AM

EL PALACIO DE LA PAPA FRITA GAINED FAME FOR A SECRET AS WELL-KEPT AS THE FORMULA FOR COCA-COLA: ITS recipe for airy crunchy delicious fried potatoes. People travel from all over the city to one of the four shops just to enjoy them.

However, El Palacio also offers an excellent variety of food traditional to Buenos Aires: *revuelto gramajo*, *milanesas*, and the unbeatable classic *bife de chorizo*.

The waiters are very friendly and seem to enjoy their jobs. The two-floored restaurant is in the classic, oft-copied style of eating establishments along Corrientes. For many generations, coming to Palacio used to be an event, something to celebrate. Their slogan is: "Where it is always time to eat," so its doors are always open and its french fries are always ready. It is worth allowing yourself to get carried away here, at any time of the day. Among office workers, actors, families visiting the city center and, of course, tourists, El Palacio keeps building on its fame and is a "must" on Avenida Corrientes.

GÜERRÍN

Pizzeria

. . . .

AV. CORRIENTES *1368* ~ SAN NICOLÁS

☎ *4371.8141*

DAILY: 7AM *to* 2AM

FOUNDED SEVENTY YEARS AGO BY ITALIAN IMMIGRANTS, WHAT BEGAN AS A MODEST FAMILY BUSINESS HAS BECOME one of the most important pizzerias in the city, with a host of employees who work at full speed to assist customers coming off the Avenida Corrientes, customers who return again and again.

The image of people eating slices of pizza at the bar of Güerrín should be on a postcard. This is the same bar where, before there were tables

in the place, people stood up eating pizza with *fainá*, accompanied by a glass of muscatel, or the delicious fried empanadas that are also a Güerrín specialty.

Many years later, the tables arrived along with the introduction of a vast range of pizzas, in addition to homemade desserts, also a distinctive characteristic of Güerrín today.

Breakfast is served from seven in the morning, and pizza and empanadas from ten until late.

LA AMERICANA
Pizzería

AV. CALLAO 83 ~ SAN NICOLÁS

☎ 4371.0202

DAILY: 7AM to CLOSING TIME

L A AMERICANA IS ONE BLOCK FROM THE CONGRESS AND THE PLAZA DE LOS DOS CONGRESOS. THIS PIZZERIA BUILT its fame thanks not necessarily to its pizza, but to its secondary business, empanadas. Come here for a quick snack. It welcomes passersby at any time of the day with a huge variety of empanadas, fried or baked.

Founded in 1935, La Americana has seen the history of Argentina paraded before its windows: from marches and demonstrations to the throngs at Eva and Juan Perón's funerals. But really, people come here to eat. Pizza *a la piedra*, tender and crunchy on top, is exceptional. Service is fast and efficient; there's no time wasted here. Draught beer, muscatel, and the house wine accompany the never-ending pace of customers—those who come in at the same time every day and those who will come on the wave of the next demonstration.

LA GIRALDA

Café

....

AV. CORRIENTES *1453* ~ SAN NICOLÁS

☎ *4371.3846*

MONDAY *to* SATURDAY: 8AM *to* MIDNIGHT

SUNDAY: 4PM *to* MIDNIGHT

TO TALK ABOUT LA GIRALDA, ONE MUST FIRST TALK ABOUT AVENIDA CORRIENTES. IT IS THE STREET OF tango *par excellence* and it is along Corrientes that tango spread out from the neighborhoods to the center of Buenos Aires. The phrase "the city that never sleeps," which unites Buenos Aires and New York, originates in the nightlife of this street. Theaters, cinemas, bookshops, and cafés marked, especially in the sixties and seventies, the rhythm of the night on Corrientes. La Giralda was among these legendary establishments, although its founders originally conceived of it as a chocolate house, that is to say as a milk bar or soda fountain, which would be open during the day for families.

Today, La Giralda is one of the most traditional bars in Buenos Aires.

It has not been remodeled and it still has old white tiles, dim fluorescent lighting, and white-jacketed waiters serving customers who gather to keep the passage of time at bay.

La Giralda is famous for its traditional hot chocolate with *churros* and for huge cups of white coffee. Under glass showcases in the bar, Parma ham sandwiches prepared with *pan de miga* or the classic Argentine *pebetes* await. Through its windows, you can see the daily come-and-go

of office workers, lawyers who hurriedly walk towards the courts, or passengers streaming into the Uruguay metro station.

But the truth is that the nighttime characters of the city—writers, outdated hippies, intellectuals, musicians—have seized La Giralda as one of their traditional meeting places in the heart of the city. They order beer and peanuts in summer and gin, coffee, or whiskey in winter and sit at small, old marble and wooden tables. La Giralda is one of the sole survivors from the golden age of Corrientes.

LAS CUARTETAS

Pizzeria

....

AV. CORRIENTES *838* ~ SAN NICOLÁS

☎ *4326.0171*

MONDAY *to* FRIDAY: 11AM ONWARD

SATURDAYS: NOON ONWARD, SUNDAYS: DINNER

L AS CUARTETAS IS A HUGE PIZZERIA WITH TWO DINING ROOMS (ONE OVERLOOKS THE STREET WHILE THE OTHER sits at the back). Here, the Argentine poet Alberto Vacarezza wrote his *cuartetas y sainetes* (quartets and comic sketches), and that is the origin of the name of this unique pizzeria. In times when "Cor-

rientes didn't sleep," artists, journalists, and writers gathered here. The neighborhood of San Nicolás has always had a legendary nightlife spirit, well expressed through tangos and in poetry.

Opposite the Gran Rex theater, an architectural landmark, and next to the Opera Theatre, where you can see national and international theatrical productions, Las Cuartetas is *the* meeting point before or after the shows. The pizza is always reliable and abundant. The place has had the same ambiance and decor for years: low marble tables with benches to share among customers and professional waiters who are great fun to watch as they carry piles of plates on their arms.

LOS GALGOS

Café

....

AV. CALLAO *501* ~ SAN NICOLÁS

☎ 4371.3561

MONDAY *to* FRIDAY: 6AM *to* 9PM

SATURDAY: 6AM *to* 2PM

B Y 1830, THE BORDERS OF BUENOS AIRES HAD REACHED THE STREET NAMED DE LAS TUNAS AT ITS WESTERN limits. De Las Tunas owed its name to the delicious prickly pear—extinct in this part of the country today. It is hard to believe that the spot where Los Galgos is located used to be a plot of farms and later

became a mere trail on which you could barely find your way. Today, it is Avenida Callao and one of the city's most important axes, and the portal to Recoleta.

Los Galgos opened in 1930 and is stuck in time, a tribute to Buenos Aires. A pair of porcelain greyhounds have been guarding the place since then, when gin fueled the tango rhythm in a fast-growing city.

Los Galgos offers good coffee, *picadas*, toasted sandwiches, beer,

and, as always, gin. However, choosing this bar doesn't have to do with eating, necessarily, but with formalities and style. It is one of those places where, off one of the busiest corners of Buenos Aires, you can step back in time.

LOS INMORTALES
Pizzeria
....

CALLE LAVALLE 746 ~ SAN NICOLÁS

☎ 4322.5493 / 4394.8532

DAILY: LUNCH and DINNER

CALLE LAVALLE, BETWEEN CARLOS PELLEGRINI AND THE AREA KNOWN AS *EL BAJO*, IS ONE OF THE FEW PEDESTRIAN streets in Buenos Aires. It used to be the street of the cinemas, where everything was marquee lights and endless queues to see the premieres of the week. Now there are few cinemas left, but you can still see hints of art deco details hidden in the façades.

The combination of cinema and pizza is as traditional as tango in Buenos Aires. And if you want to see them together (that is, pizza and tango) the best place to come is Los Inmortales, where the image of the great tango singer Carlos Gardel welcomes you with a smile at the entrance. This branch opened in the year 1966 and is still a city center landmark. Its walls are covered with photographs of the writers, actors, and singers who helped build the identity of the city—like this pizzeria—through their work. There are some who say that Los Inmortales has the best pizza in Buenos Aires. But really, this is an old debate where personal passions and the sense of belonging to certain neighborhoods merge. What is true without doubt is that the mozzarella, *fugafaina*, and calzones will have you eating in one of the most traditional places in the city center, and leave you feeling more than happy.

MAR AZUL

Bar

....

TUCUMÁN *1700* ~ SAN NICOLÁS

☎ *4374.0307*

MONDAY *to* FRIDAY: 7:30 *to* 9PM

THE POEM BY ARTURO CUADRADO, THE FAMOUS POET AND EDITOR, SAYS "BLUE SEA. BLUE SKY. WHITE SAIL ..." THIS café in the courthouse district keeps sailing with new owners just as it did sixty years ago when its first owner, a Spanish immigrant, sailed to Buenos Aires and opened the doors to this small place.

It is difficult to explain why, but the place is magical. Perhaps it is precisely because of that, since like magic, Mar Azul's charm is inde-

scribable. In this typical café and bar, white coffee, *corta-dos*, sandwiches, and the daily special give way to an apéritif hour with the bar snacks known as *ingredientes*, and wine with soda later in the night.

Men with newspapers, students from nearby universities, and lawyers from the courts chat enthusiastically while they concentrate on their reading at

the same time. Half a block from Mar Azul is the Unión Cívica Radical, headquarters of one of the two most important political parties in Argentina, so many afternoons Mar Azul is the home of political meetings where heated discussions continue late into the night.

PETIT COLÓN
Café
....

LIBERTAD *505* ~ SAN NICOLÁS

☎ *4382.7306*

DAILY: 8AM *to* 1AM

AMIXTURE OF FRENCH AND VIENNESE, WHAT MAKES THIS CAFÉ SO SPECIAL IS ITS LOCATION. RIGHT ON THE CORNER of Lavalle and Libertad, this little place is only a hundred meters from the Colón Theatre (the city's famed opera house) opposite the Palace of Justice. It has the elegant and distinguished atmosphere loved by the classical music aficionados who frequent it before and after perfor-

mances, and the necessary discretion to accommodate visitors in the legal professions. The small round tables on the pavement are reminiscent of Paris, but the classic dish for lunch, *callos a la Madrileña*, transports you to Spain. Petit Colon is where European traditions, which contributed so much to the identity of Buenos Aires, merge.

There is an extensive list of whiskies, liqueurs, and cognacs, ideal to drink before or after an opera or

ballet or simply to accompany conversations or breaks in the middle of a hectic day. Beer served alongside *ingredientes* is one of the hallmarks of the house, just as are toasted sandwiches, *traviatas*, and cakes.

Its glass windows overlook Plaza Lavalle, scene of the *Revolución del Parque* in 1890 (during which President Juárez Celman resigned and the Unión Cívica Radical was formed) and where today there is a book market specializing in legal books. The spot where the Colón Theatre stands today was once the site of Buenos Aires' first railway station. The famous train, *La Porteña*, departed from here, continued along Corrientes and terminated up in Chacarita de los Colegiales, an area that gave rise to two of the most famous neighborhoods of the early twentieth century. With some imagination and a good coffee in your hands, you can see Buenos Aires' past through the windows of Petit Colón.

PIPPO

Restaurant
. . . .
PARANA *356* ~ SAN NICOLÁS
☏ *4374.6365*
24 HOURS

PIPPO IS A REAL BUENOS AIRES INSTITUTION. THIS RES-
TAURANT HAS ALLOWED MANY GENERATIONS TO EAT OUT
during the frequent financial crises of the sixties, seventies, and
eighties. Pippo was one of the few affordable places to eat near Avenida
Corrientes. Big portions of vermicelli *al tuco* and *al pesto* were witness
to long unforgettable nights. There was a time when Pippo hardly ever
closed; its customers didn't give it time to!

Tablecloths are still made of paper, perhaps more out of tradition
than economic necessity. Pasta dishes are as tasty as different grilled cuts
of meat or *provoleta*. No choice will disappoint. At Pippo, waiters rush
from table to table skillfully carrying piles of plates. The commotion
of the place is part of its charm. As Pippo is always busy with a cross-
generational crowd, it isn't uncommon to find in the same room actors
and audience members from the same performance at one of the many
theaters lining Avenida Corrientes, or the Paseo La Plaza Theater at the
other end of the street, or groups of friends and families that round off
the day with a dinner at Pippo, perhaps one of the most fabled restaurants in the city.

RICHMOND
Café-Bar
....
FLORIDA 468 ~ SAN NICOLÁS

☎ 4322.1341 / 1653

MONDAY to SATURDAY: 7AM to 10PM

RICHMOND IS A CLASSIC, INSEPARABLE FROM THE HISTORY OF CALLE FLORIDA. SINCE COLONIAL TIMES, THE STREET has been known as one of the most exclusive in the city for its European designer boutiques and its Parisian-style buildings. It was one of the first cobbled streets and, since 1917, busy with window shoppers and pedestrians. Confectioner Richmond opened here in 1917 and was frequented by the upper classes of the city center through the twenti-

eth century as a place open both to debate and artistic creation.

It is furnished in the English style, with Chesterfield chairs, Thonet side tables, and armchairs covered in red leather, and the waiters are always very formally dressed. The dim lighting comes from bronze chandeliers that give the tearoom an old warm touch.

Many customers come in the morning for a typical continental or American breakfast. At the back of the room is the restaurant, where a pre-fixe menu is served in addition to a

variety of international dishes on the regular menu. In the basement is a pool and billiards salon where you can take free lessons or take part in tournaments.

Confectioner Richmond is well remembered for being a second home to painters such as Xul Solar and Emilio Pettoruti and for being the scene of the literary vanguard headed by Jorge Luis Borges. The young writers and journalists who formed the Florida group, responsible for the famous literary magazine *Martin Fierro*, gathered here beginning in 1924.

Even though the café is crowded all day, thanks to its legendary reputation, the hours around tea time are the busiest. Waiters weave between tables carrying trays loaded with cakes, Parma ham *traviatas*, fancy cookies, and all the accoutrements necessary to maintain the popularity of this time of the day. After that, whiskey, apéritifs, cognac, and appetizers will appear, for those who know that spending some time at Richmond not only means a peaceful moment in a busy day, but also lends a mark of style and elegance to the experience.

ZUM EDELWEISS

Restaurant

....

LIBERTAD *431* ~ SAN NICOLÁS

☎ *382.3351 / 4175*

DAILY: NOON *to* 3AM

JUST LIKE CAFÉS IN BUENOS AIRES, WHICH HAVE BIG GLASS WINDOWS THAT INVITE YOU TO DAYDREAM AND PEOPLE watch, beer halls in Buenos Aires offer refuge, privacy, and the illusion of a certain stillness of time. Zum Edelweiss is a German restaurant and beer hall which became, due to a tradition of unquestionable quality, one of the most respected and time-honored places for Buenos Aires residents. It first opened in 1907, and was located one block from its present location until the land was annexed to carve out Avenida 9 de Julio. But Zum Edelweiss stayed in the neighborhood. Since then,

it has been the lunch spot for big groups of lawyers and other customers. At night, it is the regular stop for those who come out of the Colón Theatre, and the second home of artists from the area. All the comedians from the Avenida Corrientes theaters go here. The legendary Alberto Olmedo, perhaps the best-loved Argentine comedian, even included the name of one of the dishes in his act: "What did you add to the *chambonon?*"

German specialities are the stars of the menu: *choucroute garnier* (a pork dish with sauerkraut) and fish. But soups are also striking for their simplicty. They are traditional, homemade, and served directly from the pot at the table. Desserts are generous: *carcavallo,* guavas, chestnuts in syrup.

The friendliness of the waiters and their ability to recommend the best dishes should not be underestimated. Like many of these places, Zum Edelweiss is the home of Buenos Aires' sleepless bohemians. The writer Manuel Mujica Lainez once said: "This is one of the places in Buenos Aires where I have felt close to mysterious happiness."

BAR BRITÁNICO

Café-Bar

AVENIDA BRASIL *399* (CORNER DEFENSA) ~ SAN TELMO

☎ *4300.6894*

DAILY: 24 HOURS

FOUNDED IN 1930 AS LA COSECHERA, BAR BRITÁNICO IS THE CLASSIC BAR AROUND THE CORNER, GIVING COMFORT TO neighborhood regulars or to those who return like moths to a flame. When it was threatened with modernization in 2006, its more passionate fans defended it to the end—and they won. It may have new owners, but it retains its old spirit.

Since its earliest days, it has been served by three Spanish waiters

who baptized it Bar Británico to pay homage to the British soldiers who gathered here after World War II. One of the myths surrounding the place is that the neutral name was the result of a negotiation between the Spanish waiters (known as *Gallegos* among regulars) to settle a domestic difference: one of them was a Republican and the other one was a declared supporter of Franco, and they had to alternate shifts to avoid meeting each other in the bar.

At one of the tables near the window, Ernesto Sábato wrote part of *Sobre Héroes y Tumbas* (published in English as *On Heroes and Tombs*), a book that today is among the classic works of Argentine literature. The bar, like all old bars in the city, originally had a designated section for families that was away from the saloon bar; today those white-clothed tables are reserved for the most intimate encounters.

The food is simple but honest: traditional and generous sandwiches, good coffee, classic drinks. With Parque Lezama as a backdrop behind the big windows, neighbors and regular customers are loyal to Británico for their morning coffee and newspapers, to study at in the afternoon, or to share a beer with friends at sunset. Much later, it is home to night-time tango singers who wander the area and to taxi drivers who chat until sunrise.

EL DESNIVEL

Steakhouse

....

DEFENSA *855* ~ SAN TELMO

☎ *4300.9081*

MONDAY: AFTERNOON *through* DINNER

TUESDAY *to* SUNDAY: LUNCH *through* DINNER

THIS SAN TELMO RESTAURANT IS PECULIAR IN THAT IT RESEMBLES SO MANY OTHERS OF INFERIOR QUALITY while being quite special in and of itself. When you come in, you can't help but be tempted by the grill, which is quite a sight, and once inside the dining room, a promise is made fact: there are great meat dishes to be had at El Desnivel and that's why, besides its good prices, it is always crowded. You may have to test your patience to get a table, but once the waiter rushes in to take your order, which won't be written down, you won't be sorry. Orders are never forgotten or mistaken despite the number of diners and the fast pace of the dining room.

Big tables are always full of noisy and festive parties who come to pay a visit to the oldest neighborhood in town and be among the locals. On Sundays, the restaurant's liveliness is heightened by the antiques market held nearby.

BAR EL FEDERAL

Bar – Restaurant

. . . .

CARLOS CALVO *399* (CORNER PERÚ) ~ SAN TELMO

☎ *4300.4313*

DAILY: 8AM *to* 2AM

SAN TELMO WAS THE FIRST RESIDENTIAL AREA IN BUENOS AIRES (AND HAD THE FIRST BUILDINGS TALLER THAN ONE story), with cobbled streets and bustling commerical activity. But the neighborhood changed in 1870 when prosperous families moved to the north of the city to escape an outbreak of yellow fever that decimated the population. San Telmo redefined itself after the epidemic to eventually become known as the traditional center of tango in Buenos Aires.

In spite of the changes, a few places have somehow stayed loyal to the area. Originally, in 1864, a traditional local grocery inhabited this corner. When the ownership changed, it became a restaurant and bar before a tragic story closed it for a time. Today, Bar El

Federal has returned this distinctive corner to its raison d'être. From its appearance—with the original low bar, the old bottles, and the dark wooden tables—to its variety of dishes and the charms of the café, it captures the traditional mood of this part of the city. El Federal is open all day for lunch, apéritifs, and dinner.

LA CORUÑA
Bar Restaurant

. . . .

BOLÍVAR 994 ~ SAN TELMO

☎ 4362.7637

DAILY: 7AM to MIDNIGHT

UNFORTUNATELY, THERE ARE FEW MARKETS LEFT IN BUENOS AIRES. IN THE FIRST HALF OF THE TWENTIETH CENTURY, markets were not just the standard place for buying produce and meat, but they also served as an invaluable meeting place for neighbors. The architectural jewel that is San Telmo Market is one of the last examples of the importance of local trade in the city, and La Coruña is a typical market *fonda* on Calle Bolívar.

In the morning and afternoon, it serves as a bar and café with classic bread and butter to accompany big cups of milky coffee, and a glass of wine with some nibbles at the beginning of the evening. At midday, the aromas wafting from the kitchen invite you to eat whatever is being prepared, announced on the blackboard menu. La Coruña is visited by workers from San Telmo and by those who recognize in it the authentic Buenos Aires. A few years ago, it was declared a "Bar Notable"—a historically significant establishment whose character and spirit will be preserved, along with all its original features.

LEZAMA

Restaurant

. . . .

BRASIL *359* ~ SAN TELMO

☎ *4361.0114*

MONDAY *to* SATURDAY: NOON *to* 4:30PM *and* 8PM *to* 2AM

SUNDAY: NOON *to* 5PM

PORTEÑOS LIKE TO THINK THAT THE CITY WAS ESTABLISHED ON A SPOT OPPOSITE THIS RESTAURANT, AT PARQUE LEZAMA, in 1536. (It was an effort successfully thwarted by the indigenous people, and the city was reestablished forty-four years later, farther inland.) Lezama, a simple and classic *bodegón*, invites you to daydream

about an older Buenos Aires through its large glass windows.

Quiet at midday and always crowded at night, it offers, above all, quality food. Portions are usually sized to share, like those at any restaurant priding itself in being a true *bodegón*. The waiters are notable for their friendliness and good conversation, and the prices for being accessible. The size of the dining room and the spirit of the place make it possible for groups of friends to put tables together without interfering with those who prefer some intimacy for a private meal.

On weekends, Lezama is a favorite among tourists or locals walking around San Telmo, visiting the antiques fair at Plaza Dorrego, being lured along by the capricious tango melody being played in the street.

LOS CHANCHITOS

Restaurant

....

AV. ANGEL GALLARDO *601* ~ VILLA CRESPO

☎ *4856 6535 | 4857.3738*

DAILY: LUNCH *and* DINNER

WHEN LOS CHANCHITOS OPENED MORE THAN TWENTY-FIVE YEARS AGO, LOCALS CELEBRATED. ALL THE CUTS of meat are excellent, served in very generous portions with sauces and *chimichurri*. *Matambrito de cerdo*, offal, and the traditional *asado de tira* are for two, although you can order half portions of most items. Many times this decision is actually in the hands of the waiters, who are cheerful accomplices of the customers. Another specialty is *picadas*. They are so varied in type, and the selection is so complete that many people come from all over the city to take them home. Those who can make room for dessert have great choices. Desserts are listed on the wall and I recommend not worrying about counting calories.

The rooms are noisy, like those in any popular restaurant. Laughter catches on from table to table as regular customers greet each other or wait outside for a free table while eating peanuts. You won't make a mistake if you come to Los Chanchitos, nearly opposite Parque Centenario. Locals from La Pâternal, Villa Crespo, and other surrounding neighborhoods know this for a fact.

SAN BERNARDO
Café
. . . .
AV. CORRIENTES 5434 ~ VILLA CRESPO

☎ 4855.3659

24 HOURS

I N THE EARLY TWENTIETH CENTURY, BUENOS AIRES, AND MUCH OF THE REST OF ARGENTINA, BECAME HOME TO émigrés from all over the world. That is why it is often said that the city's origin is in its ships. At the beginning of the last century, a large number of Jews chose Villa Crespo in which to settle down and gradually become citizens. These immigrants, who were mostly left-wing intellectuals, soon found in San Bernardo the perfect spot for their meetings and their recreation. Next to what used to be the biggest cinema in

the area (today it is a *"todo por dos pesos"* shop), this café and billiards and game room is steeped in history and is still a vital place for the regulars of Avenida Corrientes, just on the border with Chacarita. Important writers and editors have spent many hours at this café: Celedonio Flores, Leopoldo Marechal, the bookshop owner Manuel Gleize, the poet César Tiempo.

If you are looking for the glamour of

a Parisian café, this is definitely not the place. Style here has a more intangible quality. The large space is almost exclusively male territory. Coffee, croissants, *churros*, and milkshakes are just an excuse to be here, like a second home. In the morning, you can see men chatting, playing, discussing the daily news. Afterward, lunch awaits with quick food and daily specials: baked chicken with potatoes, *mondongo*, mince pie. Everything is fresh, honest, and generously apportioned. A long time ago, tango orchestras gave performances here that lit up the nights in Villa Crespo. Today, a picture of Carlos Gardel watches from above and ensures that the spirit here remains untouchable.

At sunset, like in all bars, whiskey leads to confessions before returning home or, in fact, before leaving, because for those who "stop by," San Bernardo is an extension of home.

CAFÉ DE GARCÍA

Bar — Restaurant

....

SANABRIA *3302* ~ VILLA DEVOTO

☎ *4501.5912*

MONDAY *to* SATURDAY: 6AM *to* 2:30AM

SUNDAY: 9AM *to* 9PM

CLOSED SUNDAYS IN WINTER

CAFÉ DE GARCÍA IS ONE OF THOSE FAMILY BUSINESSES THAT HAS PASSED FROM GENERATION TO GENERATION. Today, it is still run by the García brothers, who have retained the café's style and atmosphere that have made this corner so famous.

It opened in the center of the middle-class Devoto neighborhood in 1900. Hung around the room are icons of Argentine pop culture: a national football team T-shirt signed by Maradona, a portrait of Carlos Gardel, and old posters for Fernet-Branca, Martini, and Biltz.

Although there is homemade food at lunchtime, the specialty of the house is the *superpicada*, with more than thirty ingredients, which is served Thursday to Saturday from 8:30 in the evening. You must book a table especially for the occasion.

Café de García operates as a café all day and the billiards tables, which give the place its peculiar "frozen in time" feeling, are always available for a game.

GLOSSARY

ACHURAS: offal

ALFAJOR ROGEL: pastry filled with *dulce de leche* and topped by meringue

ASADO: a preparation that can refer to barbecued or roasted meat

ASADO DE TIRA: roast rib of beef

BACALAO A LA VIZCAÍNA: salt cod served with olive oil, garlic, onions, tomatoes, and red peppers

BARSZCZ: borscht

BATATA: sweet potato

BERENJENAS EN ESCABECHE: eggplant marinated in a sauce of vinegar, onions, carrots, and peppercorns

BIFE DE CHORIZO: sirloin strip steak; the typical cut of beef to ask for in a restaurant or *parilla*

BIFE DE COSTILLA: T-bone steak

BODEGÓN: cheap restaurant

BONDIOLA: pork shoulder

BONDIOLA A LA RIOJANA: pork shoulder in a sauce made with eggs, garlic, and tomatoes

BUÑUELOS: a typical fritter dish usually made with spinach, eggs, and spices

CALDILLO DE CONGRIO: conger eel soup

CALLOS A LA MADRILEÑA / MONDONGO A LA ESPAÑOLA: tripe and pork stew

CARCAVALLO: meringue with cream

CERDO / COSTILLITAS: pork ribs *a la riojana*: grilled and served with French fries, fried eggs, bacon, and grilled pieces of red pepper

CHURROS: sweet fritters made with milk, eggs, and sugar

COCHINILLO COMO EN SEGOVIA: suckling pig

CONEJITO A LA CAZADORA: traditional preparation of rabbit, with garlic, vegetables, white wine, tomatoes, and mushrooms

CONFECTIONER: also called a *confitería*; tea house

CONGRIOS: conger eels

COPAS HELADAS: ice cream with chocolate, strawberries, or cherries served in a glass cup

CORTADO: small coffee with a dash of milk

CHIMICHURRI: a hot sauce made with parsley, cilantro, and spices usually served with beef and chicken; each restaurant prides itself on its own recipe

CHIPIRONES RELLENOS: stuffed small cuttlefish

CHORIPÁN: spiced pork sausage sandwich

DULCE DE CAYOTE: a jam made with a variety of squash called *cayote*

DULCE DE LECHE: literally "sweet of milk"; a traditional dessert made by caramelizing sugar in milk

EMPANADAS: small pastry with savory filling
al horno: heated in the oven
con carne cortada a cuchillo: stuffed with cubes of meat
criollas: meat-filled

ENSALADA RUSA: "Russian salad" of potatoes, carrots, peas, and mayonnaise

ESCALOPES A LA MARSALA: breaded, fried meat served with a type of demi-glace

FABADA ASTURIANA: bean and bacon soup

FACTURAS: bread rolls

FAINÁ: chickpea flour pizza

FUGAFAINA: a mix of *fugazzeta* and *fainá*

FUGAZZA: pizza with onion

FUGAZZETA / FUGAZZA CON QUESO: pizza with onion and cheese

FUGAZZETA RELLENA: "folded" pizza with onion, filled with cheese

GUISO: stew

HUMITAS EN TAMALES: seasoned corn paste folded into a cornhusk

INGREDIENTES: small servings of meat and cheese typically served with drinks

LECHE MERENGADA: milkshake made with milk, sugar, and egg whites

LECHÓN: pork

LOCRO: a stew containing meat, beans, potatoes, corn, and vegetables

LOMO: tenderloin; considered the best cut of beef available (pork tenderloin is known as *lomo de cerdo*)

MARISCADA: a casserole featuring a variety of seafood

MAR Y TIERRA: a seafood and meat mixed grill; "surf and turf"

MASAS FINAS/MASAS SECAS: typical cookies served with coffee or tea; might be flavored with chocolate or dried fruit

MATAMBRE: meat roulade filled with vegetables and hard-boiled eggs

MATAMBRITO DE CERDO: a thinly sliced pork flank

MATE: tea-like infusion made from the dried leaves of an evergreen tree and typically served in cups fashioned from dried gourds

MEDIALUNAS: croissants

MILANESAS NAPOLITANAS: breaded meat often topped with cheese and tomato sauce

MOLLEJA: sweetbreads of lamb or beef

MOLLEJAS DE CORAZÓN AL VERDEO: beef heart cooked with onion

MONDONGO A LA ESPAÑOLA: a stew prepared with *mondongo*, onion, red pepper, tomato, bacon, chickpeas, and beans

PAMPLONAS: meat roulade

PAN DE MIGA: thinly sliced, crustless bread

PAN DULCE: a sweet bread eaten during the Christmas holidays

PANQUEQUES: pancakes

PAPAS A LA ESPAÑOLAS: fried sliced potatoes; french fries

PAPAS SOUFFLÉ: lightly french-fried potatoes with air pockets

PARRILLADA: mixed grill of meat and offal

PEBETES: an almost sweet, very soft bread roll *de pan negro*: brown bread roll

PECETO AL HORNO CON PAPAS: a popular cut of meat cooked in the oven with potatoes; similar to roast beef

PEJERREY GRAN PARANÁ: a white meat river fish from the Rio Paraná served with boiled potatoes

PICACHU: Buenos Aires slang for hot or spicy

PICADA/PICADA COMPLETA/SUPERPICADA: large selection of cold meats, cheeses, olives, and a variety of other finger food

PIEROGI RUSKIE: boiled dumplings filled with potatoes

PIZZA CANCHERA: pizza topped only with tomato sauce and spices

PROVOLETA: spiced grilled cheese

PUCHERO: a Spanish stew prepared with beef, bacon, chorizo, and vegetables (referred to as *puchero mixto* when prepared with chicken, as well); less frequently spelled *puchera*

PULPERÍA: a country grocery, where gauchos would gather to play cards and drink gin

QUESILLO CON DULCE DE ALCAYOTA / DE MAMÓN / DE MILE DE CAÑA: regional cheese served with sugar cane honey or confit made from the *alcayota* or the *mamón* fruit (both from northern Argentina).

QUESILLO DE CABRA CON MILE: goat cheese with honey

RABAS: fried squid rings

REVUELTO GRAMAJO: a typical dish of french fries with ham and eggs

RIÑONCITOS: kidneys
a la provenzal: in a sauce of parsley and garlic
a la veneciana: in a spinach sauce

ROTISERIA DELY: a place where food to go can be purchased

SESOS DE NOVILLO A LA PROVEZAL: cow brains served in a garlic and parsley sauce

SETAS: mushrooms
a la plancha: grilled mushrooms

SLEDZ: herring

SUPREMA MARYLAND: a dish made with breaded chicken, fried banana, french fries, and corn custard

TAPA DE MERINGUE: a meringue disk

TORTILLAS: a thick omelette-like dish of potatoes and eggs

TOSTADOS: toasted sandwich

TRAVIATA: a savory, salty biscuit served topped with prosciutto

TUCO: tomato sauce

VACÍO: meat

VITHEL THONÉ: a cold appetizer of thin slices of veal served in a capers, tuna, and mayonnaise dressing

INDEX

LA CASA POLACA
Restaurant ~ 75

LA COCINA
Home Cooking ~ 90

LA CORUÑA
Bar-Restaurant ~ 142

LA EMBAJADA
Bar-Restaurant ~ 47

**LA ESQUINA
HOMERO MANZI**
Café-Restaurant ~ 26

LA GIRALDA
Café ~ 118

LA ORQUÍDEA
Café ~ 18

LA PERLA
Cafe-Bar-Restaurant
42

LA PUERTO RICO
Café ~ 48

LAS CUARTETAS
Pizzeria ~ 120

LAS VIOLETAS
Restaurant-Bar ~ 82

LEZAMA
Restaurant ~ 144

LOS CHANCHITOS
Restaurant ~ 147

LOS CHILENOS
Restaurant ~ 102

LOS GALGOS
Café ~ 122

LOS INMORTALES
Pizzeria ~ 125

**LOS TREINTA
Y SEIS BILLARES**
Bar ~ 51

MAR AZUL
Bar ~ 126

MIRAMAR
Restaurant-Rotisería
20

ÑA SERAPIA
Home Cooking ~ 76

PALACIO ESPAÑOL
Restaurant ~ 52

PETIT COLÓN
Café ~ 128

PIPPO
Restaurant ~ 131

PUNTO Y BANCA
Pizzería ~ 79

**RECUERDO-LA
ESQUINA DE
OSVALDO PUGLIESE**
Bar ~ 30

RICHMOND
Café-Bar ~ 132

RODI-BAR
Restaurant-Bar ~ 95

ROMA
Café ~ 22

SAINT MORITZ
Bar ~ 103

SAN BERNARDO
Café ~ 148

VARELA VARELITA
Café ~ 80

VICENTE
Restaurant ~ 34

ZUM EDELWEISS
Restaurant ~ 134

INDEX

BY TYPE OF ESTABLISHMENT

ABOUT THE AUTHOR

GABRIELA KOGAN is a graphic designer based in Buenos Aires specializing in book design. Her studio has recently published *Surtido, 268 images of the Argentine Soul*; *20th-Century Graphic Advertisements from Argentina*; and *Viejo Buenos Aires*, under her imprint Del Nuevo Extremo.